Introduction

W hen I was 21, I was diagnosed with rheumatoid arthritis and lived with the fear that I might never camp again.

As a 28-year-old single mother with a new baby, my arthritis went into remission and I was determined to pass my love of nature and camping on to my little girl. I knew that I wouldn't be able to set up a tent and keep an eye on my baby, so I threw a used camper on the back of my old Ford pickup, built a crib by putting up a piece of plywood by one of the benches and headed to a private campground in the Canadian wilderness with my 11-month-old daughter.

Four years later we were joined by a wonderful man who encouraged and shared my adventurous spirit. When we had a baby seven weeks early, we bought a tent trailer to keep him off the ground and, when he was six weeks old, we took him camping with his big sister. My third child was eight months old when we moved them out of the tent trailer and took them winter RVing in a rented motorhome. We bought a trailer and to this day our fourth child and our dog just go with the flow; winter spring, summer and fall. At 16, the eldest still enjoys it when she comes with us. People often ask "How and why do you do it?" Then they want to know where to start. That is how this book came to be. It shows you how and why sleep-deprived parents take their kids RVing to get a break. It gives you the basics, the options, and some of our secrets about how to make family RVing fun, with minimal hassle and minimal thinking.

There are two parts in this RVing book. The first part covers preplanning, trip preparation, tips for camping with different ages, risk management and RV resources. The second part includes all my lists and menus as examples.

The pre-planning section at the beginning of this book asks and gives you our answers to "Why RV?" It helps you decide which RV experience suits your needs, because you will not have the same tastes or the same reasons for camping as we do. This section will give you the ideas, options and the risks of different types of trips. If you are considering renting, buying an RV or upgrading your existing one, you would want to consider these ideas before you take that step.

The 'How' section gives you step by step instructions on getting ready. There are things you will only do the first time you go, and things you will have to do every time you head out. I have a three-day countdown that I use to prepare for most trips. I could get our family of six ready for a trip in one day, but my responsibilities of chauffeur, chief chef and bottom washer for four kids don't stop while I get ready, so I break the tasks down and begin preparing three days in advance.

Tips, games, and strategies we've found useful when RVing with different ages and in groups are found in the

RVing with Kids - 12 Months a Year: The How-to Book of Family RVing

Joan van Dolder

Author: Joan van Dolder
Book design and illustrations: Dean Pickup of Dpict Visual Communications
Cover image: Drecoll, K.u.H., Plainpicture Photography

Printed in Canada by Friesens

ISBN 978-0-9784214-0-3

third section. You'll find out why we've included certain items in the lists in your workbook.

The risks of RVing with kids when using common sense are definitely manageable. Being aware and minimizing risks is covered in the 'Is it safe' section.

Finally, RV Resources covers where extra help is available, both on the street, and on-line.

You can use Part 2, which includes my lists and menus, as your workbook. You can add, delete or modify my lists to fit your tastes and circumstances. I've divided items into groups, generally arranged as items that are packed in the same area or drawer; items you might consider based on ages of the campers; and items for certain destinations. I don't expect your RV to look the same as mine, nor would I expect your tastes to be the same as mine. Remember, each trip may be different, so make a master copy, keep what you want and scratch out the rest. I have left room for you to fill in your own items.

Part of the fun of RVing is reminiscing about past trips. We started keeping a journal four years ago. Not only does it remind us of what sites we prefer at a particular campground, it preserves our funny and memorable RV adventures. (See pg. 73)

These memories are part of why we RV with our kids and this easy how-to book will help you create your memories.

As a parent, RVing slows the merry-go-round of life to a crawl. For RVing children, the crawling merry-go-round gives them the opportunity to jump off for a short time. There are not many gifts we could give our kids that are as important or enlightening.

Contents

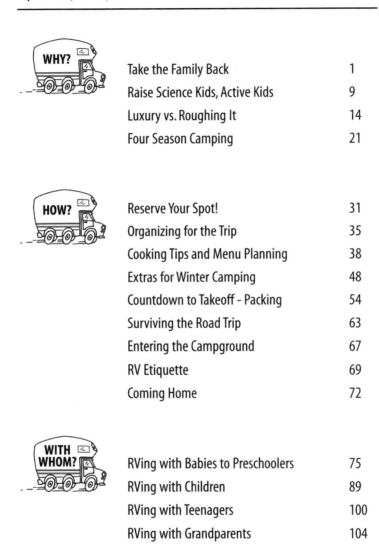

WORKBOOK

RVing with Kids 12 Months a Year
The How-to Book of Family RVing

Joan van Dolder

To escape our reality now we load up the trailer, hook it onto the Suburban, throw in the kids and the dog and drive. Sometimes we go half an hour away to a lake, sometimes further. The retreat begins the minute we pull out. The kids curl up with their blankets and either pick up a book, listen to music or put on a movie if it is dark. Bribery packs are ready to go. Phones are turned off, no computers, no facebook. My husband and I can talk or zone out knowing that we will have plenty of time to talk in the next few days.

At meal time we don't have to go back to civilization and line up at a restaurant that everyone can't agree on. We don't have to order the kids a meal only to find out they aren't hungry after one bite. We don't have to dig through boxes or backpacks to find the food and stove. We just pull over, go into the trailer and eat. We eat, we use the bathroom, and if we want to go farther, we go back to our car seats, buckle up and continue driving.

When we want to recharge ourselves and reconnect with each other and our kids, our destination is total isolation.

We'll find some secluded site on a backroad next to a creek or a recreation area and park. We don't have to set up or take down the trailer, just turn the propane on, maybe the furnace, take the bikes down, pull a few toys out and we're done. Within ten minutes we are sitting on our lawn chairs enjoying the peace and quiet. We're nodding off by the fire, drink in hand, listening to the wind come down from the mountain, blow through the trees around us and continue down the valley. The little one naps in the fresh air; the older kids explore the area, coming back occasionally for a piece of bread to tempt a bird or chipmunk to eat out of their hands.

The pace is set: slow. It is blissfully devoid of all the timelines, deadlines or schedules that fill our normal days. Work, housework and renovations are miles away and even if we wanted to, we can't do anything about them. The kids' friends are far from their minds, so mild boredom sets in and they discover their creative side as they fill their days. They play with each other and us. They read. They play games. They do crafts. Sometimes we sit around the fire, studying the glowing coals in silence or talking. Sometimes we make up stories. This is where our family reconnects, where we recharge.

Everyone has their own reasons for wanting to RV and the reasons change as children grow and life happens.

We have friends who used their RV as a base for their kids out-of-town soccer tournaments and ski competitions. When our kids grew into those activities, we joined them. While other people are trying to keep their kids quiet in the hotel room or wondering whose room their kids have disappeared into, we watch our kids bike riding or playing road hockey out the trailer window. In the loudly air-conditioned hotel room, parents are trying to converse with other parents while the kids are bouncing on the beds beside them. We get to know the other parents around a fire. At 2 a.m. in the hotel, their kids wake up to what sounds like someone jumping on the bed upstairs and can't fall back asleep. In the RV, at 2.a.m., parents and kids are asleep with fresh air blowing through the window, the only sound being the wind, the occasional hooting owl, and the soft snore of the pet dog on the floor next to them. Our hotel friends had to leave their dogs in the kennel.

We have a travel trailer, but our friends have a motor home, so they bring their RV up to the ski hill or to the soccer fields. It serves as the team shelter in rainstorms and a first aid room. They have their kitchen right there and prepare hot lunches. We can maneouver in the parking lot or downtown a little easier, but they have a place to escape for a midday nap or a hot meal at the ski hill. Both vehicles have advantages.

The motor home would be my preferred vehicle if we travelled long distances or across the country. We have friends who have family in Toronto and they often cross the country for their vacations. Their kids can sit at a table in their seatbelts and play games and even eat while they are driving. They can stop wherever they are, whenever they feel like it. If they want to change their plans and stay somewhere longer, they have everything they need with them. If all the campsites are full, they won't be out on the street. They won't have to pick the only vacant hotel left in town and pay by the hour to wiggle in a bed with dirty sheets or cockroaches. Walmart lets RVers park overnight in their parking lots for free. Sometimes when my friends are tired during the day and want to drive at night when the kids sleep, they pull into a campground or a picnic area, where the kids burn energy safely and the driver naps, killing two birds with one stone.

We RV with our kids for a variety of reasons. Mainly
- to reconnect,
- to take a break,
- to share our love of nature and
- to create special memories.

Reconnecting

Sometimes we just need to reconnect with our immediate family, but if we need to reconnect with our extended family or friends we invite them to join us.

When my 86-year-old father and 76 -year-old mother come camping with us, they use my sister's Road Trek camper van. Sitting by the campfire, we hear stories about their childhood that never would have bubbled up from their memories in any other setting. "Oma's café" opens in the morning, and upon waking, we wander over to the Road Trek in our pajamas for coffee or hot chocolate and muffins, waiting for the rest of the family to wake up.

To be able to spend a couple of days with adult brothers and sisters and their kids helps form the relationships that make life worth living. Spontaneous quality time pops up every day. While the kids were playing bocce with their uncles, my new sister-in-law saw me barbequing dinner and popped over to chat. She is not normally a backwoods person, but since she could retreat to her trailer, (for a shower and to plug in her curling iron), she is discovering both nature and the family charmers and I am getting to know her better. My brother is 12 years older than me and I never really knew him. Parked outside the community hall at a family wedding reception, my brother pitched in setting up the kids' play tent. That was the first time we had ever worked together on a project.

In today's global world, where families are scattered, friends and animals often substitute. Sharing the RV experience helps us bond with good friends with whom we normally have to pencil in an appointment just to spend an hour together. That shared time creates history and memories.

Too-much togetherness, though, can be a problem. It is especially difficult if you have little kids and have to stay under the same roof as other families. The RV gives you the flexibility to take advantage of endless opportunities to do things together, and a place to withdraw to if you need time alone or to slow the kids down.

Taking a break

It isn't only the adults that need a break from their hectic structured lives. The kids do too. So when we take a break, we also break the rules. Rules like no junk food. The kids are allowed sugared cereal on these trips and we have a treat drawer that is filled before we leave home. Our normally firm environmental rules are relaxed and we use paper plates, so we don't end up spending all our relax/play time doing dishes. We don't use alarm clocks until the last day. If we run out of underwear, we wash them in the sink, turn them inside out or buy new ones, anything so Mom doesn't have to go into town and waste her holiday in a laundromat.

Sharing our love and respect for nature

Our world is changing faster and faster and where we heard frogs near the ponds of our youth, our kids are hearing only crickets. Grizzlies are endangered. The climate is changing and lakes are disappearing. Familiar trees are dying out, being replaced by new trees. The destructive Pine Beetle has emerged as a threat to our evergreen forests.

Kids need to understand how and why the world changes. Some changes are in the hands of Mother Nature. We have no control over it. Lightning starts a fire, the forest burns and is reborn.

Some changes are caused by the actions or inaction of human beings. We are impacting change, and the rate of change, with our pollution and our intrusion into the habitat of wild animals. These are things that we do have some control over. Showing kids the direct consequences of global warming and pollution will hopefully make them *want* to make a difference.

Creating special memories of quality family time

Once of the reasons our kids love camping so much is that they have their whole family to themselves. My husband and I balance our time alone with time spent with our kids. We join in on road hockey games, take them on hiking or biking trips, create other games, and spend time listening to them. We share ghost stories by the fire with the kids, and then share a drink with each other once the kids go to bed.

Mostly we use our trailer for short weekend trips where we get the peace of the outdoors, the beauty of the mountains, and the companionship of friends and family. We don't want to travel the world in our trailer. At least, not now.

Sharing the world with your kids might be the reason you RV, though. You may want to visit fun and interesting places across the country and use your trailer as a base. Family RVing experiences can provide lots of rewarding moments whatever you decide to do.

Ask yourself:

- **Why?**

  What is your overall goal(s) or your reason(s) for RVing?

- **Who?**

  Who will be camping with you? Can they travel the distance easily? Where will they sleep? (If occasionally more people may join you, can some people sleep in a tent?)

- **How long?**

  How much time do you want to spend travelling? Do you want to spend your time travelling in the car, or relaxing at a base camp. Are you planning on travelling long distances often or staying closer to home?

  Are you planning a majority of short weekend trips or trips of longer duration?

Raise Science Kids, Active Kids

Worried scientists studying the increasing number of nature-deficient kids won't find this deficiency in RV kids! RVing in the great outdoors can foster a more active life and start a lifelong passion for nature and the natural sciences in kids, without them even knowing it. Their natural curiosity, if encouraged, teaches them about animals, plants, fossils and the circle of life.

We keep reference books on bugs, birds, insects, water pond creatures, trees, wildflowers, and even fossils in our trailer. When the kids find something, they come in and try to identify it. If it says something interesting, they look for it.

Our younger daughter, Erin, always runs around with a bug catcher and a Ziploc container or bug house. She collects all types of caterpillars and bugs and, grudgingly, lets them go to be with their family before we leave. She once found a big spider that had built a web. When we identified it, the reference book explained about how these bugs catch

food in their web. So we patiently waited and saw how it trapped a moth and then wrapped it up. Erin often finds wasp, bee and old bird nests flung to the ground and this has taught her how creative these animals can be.

Shortly after Megan learned about ant homes in Kindergarten, we went camping and she turned a stump over and saw all the rooms in the ant house. She watched the ants pull their tiny eggs on their backs and head for underground to create a new nursery. I love those Ah-hah moments, when kids make the connection to their school-work.

From going on hikes with her wildflower-loving aunt, Erin has learned to identify all types of wildflowers in the different seasons. She knows which berries the bears love and so can identify a bear habitat, a likely spot for a moose, and so on. She knows which plants were used by the natives for healing wounds. She also knows how long it takes for a wildflower to grow in the Rocky Mountains so she teaches the other kids which ones they need to respect and not step on or pick, and which are the noxious weeds.

Our little engineer, Matthew and his Dad love building things. When Matthew was three they used a huge woodpile that had been left on our campsite to make a pretend plane. We once found a number of skinny logs cut down near our campsite and the kids dragged them over to build a teepee with a tarp and bungee cords. Forts are now part of every trip. If there is a stream nearby, Matthew always tries to out-smart nature and use logs, rocks and whatever he can find to dam it.

Opportunities to develop his engineering interests pop up everywhere. When a neighbor gave us some left over baseboards for firewood, the boys built pretend guns with the baseboards and duct tape and the gun battle lasted two days. If the selection of rocks is good, he tries to build inuk-shuks, the native guiding pillars.

The different ecosystems around a stream, in the boreal forest, in the open prairies, the Rocky Mountains and around lakes offer different opportunities for learning. During the summer months, National Parks host programs on different aspects of their ecosystems. My kids will return from the program and tell me all about the pine beetle that is turning our evergreens red, how you identify the bass fish and what to do in case you encounter a bear.

The real impact of global warming touches home as their search for frogs gets more difficult and they see ani-mals that aren't normally found this far north. We talk about the trees that are dying from drought and how our forests are changing. We've watched a forest come back after being decimated by fire.

Fossil-finding has bonded the kids to their uncle. Their uncle has found them a Duckbill Platypus' forearm that they often take to school for show and tell. Now, they have researched fossils and have learned to look for dark areas on rocks to find the fossils in river banks. They have collections of jaws, teeth, and a buffalo skull. Places like the badlands in Alberta and the Burgess Shale fossil find in Field, British Columbia are fascinating for them, even though they know they can't take fossils from those places.

The kids don't only learn about science when we RV. After taking only a couple of steps, my oldest daughter learned to walk on an uneven campground, and when we returned home to flat ground, her balance had improved so much she was almost running.

With a box of sports equipment always just outside our trailer door, the kids immediately think about kicking around a soccer ball, playing road hockey, going mountain biking or even skipping. Our four-year-old boy and our fashion-conscious 16-year-old girl can hurl a football quite a distance with a wicked spiral. Using roots, rocks and plants our kids are like monkeys when they climb small cliffs. Not a camping day goes by that we haven't hiked somewhere, swam, or done some activity to burn off their energy. These activities contribute to better coordination and better fitness. More importantly, the kids learn from us that these activities are a fun way of living and sharing time with the family, and not just skills to practice if they have registered for that particular sport.

RVing and spending time outdoors with the kids is good for their confidence and helps develop other great personal qualities. Pride filled our kids' faces when they identified a bird that flew overhead. They learned patience and success from sitting quietly, waiting for a hungry squirrel to come and take a peanut from their hand. They felt compassion when they discovered a trapped fish and helped him escape back into the river.

My youngest son doesn't even realize how much he has learned from camping. He just likes that "everybody's together. The whole family!!"

Ask yourself?

- What are your child's passions and abilities?

- How can you foster that in the great outdoors?

- What interests might emerge in your child if he finds himself with relative alone time in the wild?

Luxury vs. Roughing it

Lets face it. RVing is not really roughing it. We aren't hiking with 50 lbs. of weight on our backs only to sleep on rocks under the stars.

In the $500 camper I hoisted on my truck as a single mother, I camped as primitive as a person could in an RV. Having no desire to either complicate the trip with learning the technicalities of my camper or endanger my baby by lighting the wrong thing, I basically used the trailer like a tent. I used my portable cookstove outside and used water from the campground's water pump and from my jug. I used the fridge as an ice-box, replacing ice every few days, and threw extra blankets on at night instead of using a heater. It was my shelter. We slept inside and played inside when it rained.

I could have roughed it a little bit more if I had camped in the backwoods next to a creek, boiling and treating my water and digging a hole for my bathroom. As a single mother, though, I thought a private campground would be safer for us. All I wanted was to share my love of nature and bond with my daughter in relative seclusion.

Some people prefer the opposite end of the luxury-roughing it measuring stick. They want the luxury. They opt to take their trips in one of the latest RV's with the pop-out rooms. They choose to spend their evenings sitting in front of the electric fireplace and surround themselves with the sound of their favorite satellite TV show coming from the home theatre system. Some RV's even have a washer/dryer.

The woman who won't camp because she can't take her curling iron no longer has to stay at home. In some RV's there is room to bring her whole beauty team with her. To add strawberries to their champagne, they might camp in a five-star RV resort.

Five-star resorts are already quite popular in the U.S. but more and more are popping up in Canada. They can feature swimming pools with hot tubs; petting zoos; golf courses; horseback riding; ocean sports; nightly entertainment, and restaurants. They may even have fitness and computer centres. Some resorts, not all of them five-star, cater to winter campers with ATV staging areas, cross-country ski trails, and ski hills.

Typically you have to purchase or lease property to park your RV in a resort, though some have spaces for transients passing through. The long-term commitment means people decorate their lots with patios and gardens and a sense of community develops.

Of course you can mix and match these luxury/roughing it factors. We have a friend who has a basic trailer and leased her spot in a gated RV resort about ninety minutes from town. She stays out there with her kids all summer and her husband drives out whenever he can. They have full hookup so water and power are not an issue. She doesn't feel confident enough to pull the trailer, so when she goes to the resort or goes home again, and her husband isn't there, she relies on the resort operator to bring the trailer to or from the storage yard.

My friend wanders to the coffee shop for a latte after a morning of golf, and goes to sit by the pool while an activities coordinator takes her children to a BMX track, or off to do a craft. After dinner her kids head to the basketball courts or the recreation room where they can hook up their Gamecubes to the TV. The kids also take horseback riding lessons and swimming lessons at the resort in the summer and in the winter, the family goes out to use the ATV staging area or cross country ski trails.

Other friends go the other route. They have the ultimate RV and head for the woods with their ATV and fishing rods or with their skidoos in the winter. The husband heads off during the day with the kids and the wife relaxes, listening to music or watching TV and reading. They use their generator to keep the power up and drive into town every four or five days to get water, and dump the sewage.

Our own trailer is comparatively primitive and we like it that way. In the summer we use the trailer's water and washroom, depending upon where and how long we are camping, but in the winter, our bathtub stores the snowsuits and mittens. We prefer to cook outside in the summer, on our portable cook stove or over the fire. The food seems to taste better and we find it more enjoyable. In the winter, we cook our bacon or smelly meats outside on a cook stove on a nearby picnic table, so as not to attract animals into our trailer and we use our microwave, oven or stove inside for cooking other foods.

When we first started RVing with the kids I made them read, draw or do paper-based games in the car when we drove, staying away from technology. The smartie game (see Surviving the Road Trip chapter) was their favourite. I would only start it when we were getting closer to home, and the restlessness reached its peak. They loved the game and it sure killed time.

I like to read on the drive but for the first few years I would continually be interrupted when they told me a story, asked me to sharpen a pencil, spell or define a word, get a snack or stop a fight.

I would like to say we are still electronic-free and that my kids spend all their spare time reading, playing games inside or outside or creating things with odds and ends they found outside and in the craft box. That was my intention. They would say that is primitive now.

When the kids got older, they got MP3's and Game Boys and although I didn't want the kids playing them or listening to them at the campsite, they did make the drive a little bit quieter and I was able to read my book. At first, the electronics had to stay in the car. I wouldn't let them play with their electronics at the campsite.

When we started winter camping, the daylight often ended before we left town at five or six p.m. so they couldn't read in the car. We agreed to get a portable DVD to entertain the kids on the trips. I have to admit, I liked it. It was the most peaceful trip I have ever taken with four kids in the back. I fell asleep and they didn't even wake me to ask to go to the bathroom until the movie was over. My husband and I could talk and my little one would quietly fall asleep before the movie ended.

The world without electronics was something I strived for, but after four kids and hundreds of trips, I've relaxed into reality. Today, my kids bring the DVD along in the summer and bring all their electronics into the trailer. They do watch an occasional movie and play their Game Boys. My teenager stays in touch with her friends sometimes, texting on her cell, but if we suggest a road hockey game or to do something else, they almost always put it away and join us. I justify the electronics because the trip is about kicking back and I guess that is their way of unwinding.

Our destinations vary from luxurious to semi-primitive, depending on the trip and our state of mind.

In the summer we usually go to unserviced but reasonably populated campgrounds for a number of reasons. The first one is safety. In the backwoods the kids have to stay really close when biking etc., because of wild animals. In campgrounds, the kids can go a little farther. The Parks people warn you if wild animals are in the area and if the kids are riding around the loop, you can usually see them. Also, there are always campers where they can go quickly for safety if a wild animal appears. As the kids get older we are starting to return to more remote campgrounds.

Another benefit of the more populated campgrounds is that the kids almost always meet a new friend and have someone to play with. My oldest son keeps an address book of all the friends he has met while camping. He has the intention of staying in touch, and so gets their phone numbers and addresses, but unfortunately, life happens after that and he rarely makes the call.

The National Parks' campgrounds often have educational nature shows in the summer. They are put on by parks staff and our kids also really enjoy that.

We choose the unserviced sites in the summer because we never plug in the trailer then.

The serviced areas within our favorite campgrounds are areas we stay away from in the summer because they don't offer very much privacy. In the summer season they fill up like parking lots with very large RV's that usually have generators. Although most campgrounds have rules for when Rvers can turn their generators on, the noise takes away from our serenity. We prefer more trees and less people over power, water and sewer hookups.

What little power we use comes from our battery and a solar panel that we hook up. The long sunny days mean we can live without plugging the trailer in for at least four or five days if we are careful. Because we love being outdoors, we even cook most of our meals over a fire or outside on our old Coleman cook stove.

In order to camp four or five days without having to move the trailer, we try to use the campground's washroom and showers during the day but at night and for emergencies our trailer washroom works well. In some campgrounds where there are outdoor hot water taps, I will fill my dishwashing tub with the campground's water too, if I am not parked too far away. I tend to use our tap water for cooking though.

On longer holidays we try to take a couple days at an RV resort with swimming pools and such. Depending on the lakes we have been to, our kids look forward to a heated, clean pool.

In the winter we stay in full-serviced winter campgrounds. Though they are the same parking lot we avoid in the summer, there are very few people staying in them in the winter, so the road becomes our private road hockey rink.

We don't use the water or toilets in our trailer all winter. Instead, we take advantage of the empty but clean public washrooms and showers. We also take advantage of the power hook-up. We plug in an electric heater and throw down a rug and the furnace rarely kicks in. With power, we can also use our microwave and if we had a really tiring day we might plug in the DVD player for a family movie night.

Ask yourself

- What type of a trailer do you want or have?

- Do you want to have the luxuries from home with you?

- Do you want to experience a less complicated, more natural existence?

- What types of places would you camp most often?

- Do you enjoy the isolation and serenity of the backwoods?

- Do you enjoy the relative privacy of a trailer surrounded by easily accessible organized activities and people?

- Are you concerned about security? Does a gated community appeal to you?

- How old are your kids?

- How long will you camp at a time?

- Will you camp in the winter?

Four Season Camping

As you clean out your camper and put away the sand pails and shorts, stop! The season doesn't have to end when you pour the winterizing chemicals in. We throw in a cozy rug and slippers along with our snowsuits, hockey sticks, and skis and we extend the camping season right through the year. It gives us more value for our RV money and new and exciting family adventures.

Winter camping with four young children may sound extreme, irresponsible and insane, but when you do it the right way, you only have to have common sense and an average-to-high adventurous spirit and you will find serenity, sanity and much more.

No, we don't sleep in the snow cave our kids built or freeze our backsides while going to nature's outhouse. Our family can be found cozy and warm inside our trailer.

Our secret is winter campsites in the Rocky Mountains. They are, in fact, the same places we wouldn't dream of camping in the summer, because they are parking lots packed with 40-foot RVs whose generators remind you of when you were lost behind the rides at a carnival. But, in the winter they are empty lots, well cleared, they have warm bathrooms (some even have showers) and they also have plug-ins for your trailer.

Sure, you have to plan ahead a little bit. You don't want to be pulling a trailer in freezing rain or when a blizzard is predicted. You don't want to be outdoors when it is -30 C.

With appropriate layers, my family enjoys camping as long as the daytime high is at least -15 C.

I'll admit it. I thought my husband was insane when he first suggested winter camping. We had camped a number of times in the late spring and early fall in our tent trailer and I found some nights were just too cold.

Our kids didn't like winter. Between all of their activities, I suppose they didn't have time to discover how to enjoy winter. The first snowfall of the year might bring them out for a snowball fight, but generally they would much rather stay and play indoors.

My husband was smooth. He suggested we rent a motorhome to go winter camping. The kids loved the thought of camping in a real motorhome instead of our tent trailer and begged me to agree to it.

We did our first winter camping trip when our third child was a toddler. We rented a motor home, loaded it in the cold (I've since learned better) and picked up our oldest daughter at school. I am sure that when the teacher looked out the window as we pulled up in the motorhome, he thought about calling Social Services. It turned out to be quite an adventure.

We booked a spot at Mount Kidd in Kananaskis and turned onto the dark Kananaskis highway in a blinding snowstorm. The signs on the road were blasted with snow and we had to stop and brush them off to find the turnoff

Pros and Cons of Our Favourite Winter Campgrounds

Jasper - Wapiti Winter Campground is like camping in Europe. It is a parking lot with trailers side-by-side, but there is a natural toboggan hill next to it. When it is not busy, it is great, but more skiers tend to camp here throughout the winter because it is so close to Marmot Basin. In the spring and fall, though, they open a few loops of unpowered sites, so we bring extra propane and those have become our favorites during those seasons.

Banff - Tunnel Mountain Campground is excellent even in the dead of winter. It is never too crowded, has a splendid view and the kids love the public waterpark across the street.

Lake Louise - Lake Louise Campground is nice and very close to Lake Louise Ski Resort but bring earplugs, the train runs right beside it.

Kananaskis - At Mount Kidd, the hot tub and an activity centre is a real bonus if you are crowded, or in a group. There is skating, tobogganing and cross-country ski trails up at the Village of Kananaskis and Nakiska Ski Resort is close by. The campground has cable hookups and great rates for long-term winter campers, too!

into the campground. Trying to find a spot in the dark we came across another crazy adventurer who had decorated his spot with Christmas lights.

Although the forecast was supposed to be only -15°C. at night and -3°C. during the day, the mercury dipped to -25°C. that night and the furnace ran constantly. A lot of cold air came through the front windows and we were beginning to question our sanity but our doubts vanished the next morning.

We awoke to the fresh snow glistening in the blinding sun. It stretched to the base of the mountain, untouched, except for the occasional animal track. The kids delighted in being the first to break the unending blanket of snow. There eyes lit up when they discovered the first set of animal tracks and they raced in to find our animal tracks book to identify them as deer hoofprints. We joined them on a morning walk as we hunted for more tracks on snowshoes.

In the afternoon we headed up to the Village at Kananaskis and tobogganed. Sleigh rides were running for hotel guests, and we joined in. We headed into Banff for the evening to the public waterpark and the kids were exhausted by the time we returned.

The next day, we threw our kids outside in the morning and watched them slide down the snow piles created by the snowplows. Then they pulled out the hockey sticks and played road hockey on freshly cleared roads before we headed up to Nakiska for an afternoon of skiing. A soak before dinner, in Mount Kidd's hot tub at the campground, finally exhausted the kids and the early darkness meant a quiet night in the trailer. We pushed a movie into our little TV-VCR and the kids were asleep before the first half was over.

One final adventure before we ended our weekend of winter was a hike in Johnson Canyon, just west of Banff. Though I love waterfalls in the summer, in the winter they have their own magic. The frozen waterfalls danced like the northern lights as the melted water crashed behind the icy crust. Also, the changing daylight on the canyon walls brought out different rock colours as light and shadows played on the thin layer of ice formed from the spray and mists.

We have since discovered that every waterfall handles winter differently. Maligne Canyon's thundering falls, near Jasper, grow silent and the rocky cliffs mimic the falls with dramatic frozen ice sculptures created from slow trickles on the sides of the canyon. Near the 5th bridge, for a short period during the winter, the water flow freezes, drops and freezes again, giving you the opportunity to do an "Ice Crawl" between the two levels of ice.

Winter RVing can round out a weekend of dog sledding, ice fishing, or ski-dooing if those are your passions. The long evenings can be filled with old-fashioned entertainment: games, books, crafts or even the oft-forgotten art of conversation. Early sunsets mean the kids can pull out the telescope for some star gazing and still make a reasonable bedtime. The clear cold nights in the dark mountains make the stars brighter than at home.

If we get a surprise cold day, a movie or a bowling alley in town might be our destination. Instead of showering in the campground, we sometimes hit the local pool just before bedtime. In Banff, the hot springs or the public waterpark in the hotel across from Tunnel Mountain campground is another way to have fun getting clean before bed. If the day has been busy, the microwave is standing by for a meal or a fast, warm bedtime snack to ward off the meltdowns.

The key to enjoying a winter weekend is keeping warm, and knowing that a warm place is immediately accessible, especially when you have little ones. Having a motorhome, which we brought to the toboggan hill and to the ski hill, meant anytime they were cold, they could have a cup of hot chocolate in a warm place.

Protecting Our Young Ones

The protective instinct is naturally in high gear with the birth of a new baby, but my husband met his match when we went camping in Jasper with our six-week-old baby. On an early spring morning, he stepped out of our tent trailer to face a charging elk.

Many thoughts must have crossed his mind. Should he jump back in the tent trailer, protecting himself but endangering his family? How strong is canvas anyway? Should he run from the elk, drawing her away from his family? If the elk caught him, would she just step on him and crush his insides, or would she eat him? Do elk like human meat? Does he have a clean pair of underwear?"

His paralysis seemed to have an effect on the elk who stopped metres away. My husband reached for a rock: the elk tensed ready to leap. My husband froze and then moved slower: the elk watched him.

We watched the standoff from behind the paper thin bug screens, petrified, unable to make a sound. The elk stepped forward: my husband threw a rock in front of him and the elk backed up. The elk stepped forward again: my husband threw another rock and the elk backed up again. The dance continued.

Just as they were beginning to respect each other's space, a German tourist came out of the bushes across the field and the elk charged at him. The tourist was chased around the field and ran straight into our campsite where Adrian stood with a rock raised.

The elk stopped. The elk looked over his shoulder to a patch of long grass behind our trailer and a newborn baby fawn, still wet from birth, peeked out at his mother with worried eyes.

The elk looked back at Adrian and their eyes met with understanding. Our new baby was inside the trailer and Adrian would do anything to protect him.

The elk allowed my husband to pull up the awning and we left the new family in peace.

If you are not quite ready for that, try extending the camping season into the fall. While the kids paint rocks around a warm fire, I bring out a sketchpad. The Rocky Mountains in the fall and spring show their true identities as the first and last snow packs reveal their cliffs, crevasses and plateaus, giving each mountainside a pronounced and distinct three-dimensional character which is unimaginable in the summer. Below the rocky peaks around Lake Louise in the fall, spectacular patches of gold tamaracks brighten the green carpet of evergreens and are definitely worth hiking to while the trails are still dry.

Your fall afternoon nap in a Rocky Mountain campground might be cut short by the unforgettable bugling of elk in the next campsite. The call begins the mating dance of the elk in the Rocky Mountains.

The chance to see wild animals increases when the snow line advances down the mountain as winter approaches. In the spring, since the snow is still covering the animals' food source up high, the chance of seeing the new forest babies goes up. One spring, a fawn was born overnight, right behind our trailer at a campground near Jasper.

Another spring we discovered a comparative trickle was all that flowed in place of the wild river that raced by our favourite campground in the summer. After being pounded by continuous rapids through the hot days, the exposed rocks revealed Mother Nature's elaborate carvings, and patiently waited for the snowmelt to pound into them again.

When ski season nears its end, we are able to hit the slopes on Marmot in the morning and bike ride to the Jasper Park Lodge from the Wapiti campground for a hot chocolate in the afternoon.

You don't have to jump into winter camping with both feet. Pick a fairly warm wintery weekend or begin by extending your camping season into the fall and/or spring to discover the seasonal magic in your favourite RV summer haunts.

The magical stillness of a winter wilderness will remind you that there are still places where time crawls in this world.

Ask Yourself

- What is your sense of adventure?

- Can you be flexible if the weather turns?

- Do you have the right clothing and boots?

Reserve Your Spot!

Reservations

It used to be that when you went RVing or camping, you would leave for your favourite campground after work on Friday and you would usually get a spot . Then our population grew and you had to arrive early Friday afternoon. Then, before long, if you weren't there early Friday morning, you were out of luck. Then Thursday. Then Wednesday.

Reservation systems are now in place at most campgrounds and when you have kids, it is something you will want to take advantage of. I remember many a night we would be driving in the dark from campground to campground with bickering, tired and hungry kids who were sick of travelling, trying to find a place to park. We would end up in a field with no firepit, and young kids partying in their campsite right outside our door.

Now even if we are delayed - which we often are with kids - the campground will hold our spot either until a reasonable time at night or until the next day.

Reserve ASAP

Reservations can be made for camping sites often up to the day before you arrive but it is best to reserve as far ahead as possible. National campgrounds, provincial campgrounds and even private campgrounds can fill up quickly, especially on long weekends. People will book their sites as soon as reservation lines open and for some campgrounds, that means on January 2, summer long weekends fill up. If you are thinking you might want to stay an extra day, book it. You can cancel out of a day, usually for free or a small charge. If you are already there and you want to stay an extra day, they might ask you to move to another site or ask you to leave if there is no room. Some campgrounds in Alberta are now requiring that you reserve in person, to show more commitment.

Short notice

Reservations can be made for camping sites often up to the day before you arrive. It is worth trying even the most popular destinations on long weekends in case cancellations at the last minute make spots available.

Last minute

When we decide to go camping at the last minute and we don't have a reservation, we consider a number of options. On a summer weekend we try to get to a campsite as early in the day as possible and as early in the week as possible. If we don't get in, we can sometimes get a spot with no services or we go into overflow camping the first day and line up very early the next morning for any available spaces.

We might also choose to camp at one of the province's recreation areas or in one of the smaller no-service campsites in the National Parks. They often operate on a first-come, first-served basis, and the majority of RVers who stop there are moving through. Usually there are spots, especially if you get there mid-afternoon. Sites are hardest to find on a weekend, so unless you have a reservation, I would recommend that if you already have a good spot, stay put.

If you are camping at a public or private campground by a lake, they often don't have overflow camping, so it is more important to get there earlier in the week or call before you leave and see if there is a space they can hold for you.

Serviced or unserviced

When you call to reserve a site, the campground operator will ask you the length and/or type of unit you are travelling with so they choose a large enough spot for you. Then they might offer you a choice of three different types of sites. The first is full service which means they provide the facilities for you to hook up your trailer's water, sewer and power. Your second choice is power-only sites, and your third is unserviced sites. Although full service sites may be more convenient, you may lose out on serenity and privacy in the summer which are often more abundant in non-service sites. You need to decide which type of site you want before you reserve.

Fire pit

There are some sites without fire pits, especially in full service sections, so if you want the option to have a fire, make sure you ask. There is often an extra charge for a fire permit, and although most places supply firewood, some charge a small fee for it.

Extras

When we go to a campground, we walk around and discover the sites we like; by a creek, near the playground, near a bluff or near the showers and washrooms. In our Camping Journal we record these site numbers, and when we call to reserve, we ask if we can have that site. They usually can't promise, but they often make the effort to get us our favorite spot.

Remember to take it easy on yourself

Forgive yourself if you forget anything and go with the flow. Halfzeimers (as opposed to All-zheimers) and arriving late are the two things people can count on from sleep-deprived parents. If someone complains, tell them to do it themself!

Organizing for the Trip

When travelling with kids, you need every inch you can find in your trailer, so organizing your camper to make the most of space is one of the first things you need to do. Different numbers of kids, different interests and tastes, mean your trailer won't look anything like mine, but here's my routine.

Modified KISS rule

I always follow my version of the KISS Rule which is "Keep It Small for Space." Choose pots that fit into each other. Use a dishpan that fits snugly into your sink. Take small spice containers. Choose stacked chips like Pringles instead of the big bags. Use equipment that serves two purposes whenever you can. Buy a two-litre carton of juice and then mix concentrated juice in the empty carton when you finish it.

Tote tricks

We have four kids and bringing six duffel bags of clothes made the trailer look chaotic. Also zipping and unzipping and trying to fix broken zippers because the kids crammed too much in them was almost as painful as natural childbirth.

I measured the space under the bench and did the math to find out what shape and size six containers would have to be to use every inch. Opening the bench can be disruptive if someone is trying to sleep on the bed or playing on the table, so, unless it is an emergency, I only open the bench and take clothes out once a day when I make the bed or set up the table.

Kill closet clutter

The tall closet in our trailer used to be really unorganized. The jackets hung down and everything was stuffed in below them. I bought one of those plastic two drawer units and placed it on the bottom. It is narrow enough for the adult coats to hang along side, but all the kids coats hang over top without touching. I can use the two drawers for the socks and underwear that I want accessible. Another option is to put peg board on the sides of that closet and slide in shelves in at the height you need.

Stack with racks

To avoid a food avalanche when you reach for the spaghetti sauce at the back of the cupboard, you might want to buy extra racks for the kitchen cupboards. I find them especially handy for stacking canned goods and Tupperware containers full of sugar, hot chocolate mix or spices. Line the racks and cupboards with rubbery shelf liner and your food is less likely to fall out.

Brace lose objects

Small springy curtain rods can be used to hold items back for travelling. That way when you stop and open the fridge or cupboard, everything that shifted doesn't fall out.

Convert unused beds

We have a bed above our couch that we never fold down. By taking the mattress out, we have found room for our telescope and much more.

Washroom wisdom

In the bathroom I use one of those travel toiletry bags that hang. I found a three-pocket one in an old suitcase and it now hangs on the towel rack in the RV bathroom. It is more accessible than leaving things under the counters. One pocket is for all of our toothbrushes and toothpaste and the others are for shampoo, brushes, anti-perspirant and make-up. It zips up so nothing will fall out when you travel and you can carry it to the shower without dropping things.

Smelly laundry

Dirty laundry needs to go in a green garbage bag which we keep in the shower stall. YOU MUST MAKE SURE THAT EVERYTHING THAT GOES IN THERE IS DRY OR IT WILL GROW MOULD. Unfortunately, the smell that grows in that bag is enough to gag anyone, but bleach for colours gets it out at home.

Shrinking children

When they are small you can sleep more kids sideways on beds, but sorry, I don't know how to make kids smaller. I have tried to get them to shrink and be babies again, but to no avail. . .

Cooking Tips & Menu Planning

I used to belong to a gourmet hiking group. You'd never know it. I am not a great cook. Some would say that I am a better smoke alarm tester.

My kids know that, when I am cooking in the trailer, they have to grab kitchen towels and swing madly in front of the smoke alarm to turn it off before the park warden evacuates the campground. So my tips are not for gourmets, they are simply methods of cooking that I found works better when you are RVing with different ages of kids.

Cooking Methods

Best choice with babies or winter RVing: Microwave or oven

When the kids were little, I didn't want to be cooking over a fire with them around, so my menus were full of quick meals

38

that took as little work as possible. In the summer, or if you aren't plugged in, the oven works great for frozen dishes which are quick and easy to heat up, especially for a cooler, action-packed, hungry-kid day. The oven can be dangerous if you have kids or toddlers moving around and playing in the trailer without your supervision, so kick them outside or prepare to stay in and keep them safe. In the winter or whenever you are plugged in, you can use your microwave for reheating leftovers or making hot drinks to warm the kids up fast.

Foods we often cook in our microwave or oven

- lasagne
- chicken wings
- French fries
- hot chocolate

Advantage: Reduce Cleaning – Use foil trays in the oven, and re-use them to put leftovers in the fridge, or for the next meal.

Best choice with toddlers: Cook-stove outside

Cooking on a cook stove outside is a good choice if you want a fast meal, or don't want to heat up the trailer. It is also a good choice if your kids are outside and you want to help keep an eye on them and keep your partner company, or if your kids are inside playing rather loudly or wildly and you need a safe place to cook and a break from the noise. I just like cooking in the fresh air.

Foods we often cook outside on our cook-stove

- Bacon and smelly meats (so animals aren't attracted to the smell inside our trailer)
- Coffee

- Spaghetti or noodles
- Beans and wieners
- Soups
- One-pot stews
- Boil in a bag meals.

Disadvantage: Extra cleaning – Dirty pots are a negative outcome when using the cook stove. If you've burnt something in a pot and you are having difficulty cleaning it,

throw it on the cook stove with water and dish soap and boil it for a bit. The burnt gunk soon scrapes off easily. Because I don't want to use too much water, I use paper towels to wipe as much off as I can before washing.

Best choice with older kids: over the fire

All kids love to have a fire, so once they understand the danger and you can trust them, you may want to cook over the fire and get them involved. Younger kids can help collect the wood and older kids can chop it. Building a nice cooking fire is a skill we are gradually teaching our older kids. All the kids can help prepare the foil packs, desserts, or pizzas that will cook on the fire.

Oil the foil – If your food sticks to the foil, try rubbing the inside of the foil with margarine before putting the food on it. For those on a diet, like me, sticking wax paper between the foil and food also works.

Firepits – Because firepit sizes vary we cook our food over a fire in two ways. We have a round grill from an old barbecue that fits in those round fire pits. I use metal wire where one end is tied to the grill. The other end is wrapped around heavier pieces of wood and hang outside the firepit to act as weights. Wrap the wire around the wood until the desired height of the grill is achieved.

Homemade grill – We have a steel colander with holes in it that I use as a raised grill. I simply poke metal skewers through holes across the top and put a grill, or foil pack or a piece of foil with food on it.

Fire boxes – The grill on top of a fire box can be a perfect spot to throw foil on and grill a hamburger, steak or cook pancakes. Corn cobs and potatoes can go inside on the coals. If the grill gets too hot, you can throw rocks on top and raise your cooking surface higher.

Foods we often cook on the fire

Along with basics like steak, burgers, hotdogs and pancakes, here are a few of our favorite and most interesting fire-cooked meals:

- **Chicken salsa:**
  Put salsa on a piece of foil. Lay a chicken breast on it, and add salsa on top. Wrap the foil around it twice, throw it on the fire, at 10 minutes flip over for another 10 minutes and enjoy!

- **Corn cob:**
  Soak corn in the husks in water and then throw on the fire. It will cook and not burn in about 15 minutes. Try using cream cheese as a topping instead of butter and salt.

- **Turnovers or pies:**
  Use cooking irons, like a cast-iron sandwich maker on weiner sticks (available at most camping stores), to make turnovers or pies with pre-made dough and pie filling. Use the irons for hamburgers or scrambled eggs.

- **Pizza:**
  Use soft tortilla shells or wraps and have kids spread out pizza sauce, toppings and mozzarella. Put the pizza on the grill and cover with a foil tent. It is done in 10 minutes.

- **Baked and mud potatoes:**
  Coat potatoes in wet mud and throw it on the fire. The mud will dry and crack off and the potato will cook.

- **Cleaner s'mores:**
  Bring waffle or sugar cones or tortillas and fill them with chocolate chips and little marshmallows. Wrap it in foil, heat on the fire and it won't be so messy. Nutella or Caramilk are options instead of chocolate chips, and for Reese's Pieces fans, add peanut butter.

- **Banana splits:**
  Slice an unpeeled banana lengthwise, almost all the way through. Squeeze mini-marshmallows and chocolate chips in the slice. Wrap in foil and cook on the fire until chocolate melts and banana is hot. Yum!!

- **Bannock:**
  Have fun experimenting with bannock. All you need are flour, water, cinnamon and maybe some raisins. Try different textures and wrap it on a clean, but wet stick. Hold it over the fire and learn why it's a favorite of the natives! Hint: Having butter and brown sugar to dip it in makes it even better!

Biggest Advantage of Fire pits – Use and re-use foil and you'll have no dishes to clean!!!!

Menu planning and grocery list tips

You eat tomatoes - I eat tomAtOs. Menu planning is such a personal thing that my menu samples in the back will be of no use, except to see how I set up my lists and get everything into the trailer. I use a six-step process.

1. Count the number of meals you will have while you are away; how many breakfasts, lunches and dinners. I can get up to almost four days of food in my fridge and more in my cupboard. Food is more expensive the farther you are from the city, and seems to go up 50% as you cross National Park gates. I know I will have to get milk every two days, so I plan to restock with a bigger shopping trip on the fourth day if we are staying longer.

2. Decide what you will eat for main dishes, side dishes, and desserts. Consider the size of your freezer. Will it fit all the frozen food you wanted to bring?

3. Start your list for each meal, thinking of EVERYTHING you will need on the table. My kids eat their spaghetti different ways, so I need sauce, ketchup and butter with parmesan when I have spaghetti. As you move on to your next meal, if you have the same item, don't put it on your list again.

4. Go through your cupboards and grab all the dry goods on your list and put them in a tub to unload in the trailer. Scratch them off your list as you put them in the tub. If you only have a little bit of something that you will need, leave it in the house and leave the item on the list to buy. When your trailer comes home, pack the dry goods where they belong.

5. Go through your freezer and fridge and put all items you will need, including condiments you have already shrunk in small containers, in bags to grab once the trailer comes home and the fridge and freezer are cold. Put check marks by them to show you have them, and cross them off only when they are in the trailer.

6. Once the trailer is home, plugged in and the fridge and freezer are chilled, go shopping and buy the remaining items on the list. Deposit them directly into the trailer where they belong. Move the fridge and freezer items that are still in the house into the trailer as well.

Random preparation thoughts

Stick to Favorites – I have about 5 to 7 dinner entrees that I cook over and over, because I know my kids will eat them and they are easy and fast. When I go camping, I stick close to what's familiar with a few extras. Since we eat generally pretty healthily at home, we treat ourselves to foods we don't usually buy such as sugared cereals, pops or some snacks as extras to make camping an even more special occasion for the kids. If you break the rules at home, you may want to use this opportunity, when you aren't near a grocery store, to eat healthily. If healthy food is all you have, that is what everyone will have to eat!

Re-use menus – I save my menus and re-use them and the accompanying grocery lists to save time. See samples of my menus near the back of the book.

Pre-cook meals – I also try to do some pre-cooking to save time on the trip. I might make a really big roast the week before and save the leftovers to make a beef dip on the trip. Everytime I make chili I freeze some and I might pull out a meal's worth for a camping trip. If I have to cook hamburger during the week, I cook extra for spaghetti sauce or tacos on the trip.

Rinse before you go – To save water in the trailer, I rinse all the veggies and fruit before I go.

Summer treats – Choose Mr. Freezes over popsicles or ice cream in boxes. If they thaw on the trip, or for some other reason, you can refreeze and it won't make a mess or taste bad. It can also double as a handy ice pak if someone gets hurt!

Shrink condiments – Use small Ziploc containers for ketchup, mayonnaise, and other things you don't need a lot of. You will need the room for fresh veggies and fruit.

Mix in but don't boil plastic bags – When cooking you can minimize dirty dishes by mixing food in Ziploc bags as much as possible. Don't boil food in a plastic bag, though. The manufacturers don't recommend it and believe it may pose health risks. There are nylon bags being made that can be boiled with food in but they aren't available in most grocery stores.

Breads first – Although you need to be flexible with your schedule and hunger level, plan for meals with bread or buns on the first or second day, because they don't stay fresh, especially if they are in a cupboard on a hot day. Banana Splits should be done on the first night too or the bananas go black. Keep dry goods like Mac n' Cheese for meals at the end of your trip.

Fancy Drinks – If you like fancy drinks, buy pre-made drinks. Ceasars come pre-made in individual cans, and for connoisseurs who are not easily offended, wine can be bought in a tetra-pak.

Eating outside – Rather than making a lot of trips, I use a cafeteria style tray to bring all cooking utensils and food for meals eaten outside. The tray can also be used to bring dishes, drinks and the portable cutlery container outside and back in again.

Boom!

NEVER EVER THROW AN UNOPENED CAN OF FOOD ON THE FIRE!!
We saw a can of beans explode in the campsite next to us. Ow!

Extras for Winter Camping

To truly enjoy winter camping, you have to be prepared for the worst, and hope the weather forecaster's positive predictions aren't wrong.

Any hard-sided RV is eligible for winter camping. We have a 23' 2001 travel trailer and it works beautifully.

We plug our hard-sided travel trailer in and our electrical heater and fan instantly heats it up; most nights we don't even turn on the furnace. We plug in our microwave, a luxury reserved for winter, to make quick hot meals. We don't risk having water freeze in our pipes and often fill our water jug with hot water from the campgrounds' bathrooms instead of boiling it.

Issues: Pop-outs

Pop-outs also work, but there are some weaknesses. I've been told that an electrical slide works better in extreme weather than the electric/hydraulic one, but they both should work in most conditions. The concern is that ice may form on the slide. If it does, you need to wipe off the snow, otherwise the ice will pass under the rubber blade that wipes water off during closure. Then the ice will melt inside the trailer and that could damage the walls or floors.

Having talked to winter campers with pop-outs, they tell me they don't lose heat in the walls or the connections which are insulated and close like a car door . The ceiling of the pop-out is where they think the cold air comes in. One pop-out RV owner said he just used an extra heater and was fine on a -20 Celcius night.

Issues: Windows

Although we don't do anything to our windows, we did find that you need to hang a blanket or insulation sheet across the inside of the big windows in the front of Class A motor home, or use the window insulation plastic film. The Class A motor home looks like a bus with no bed over the driver's seat.

A bigger problem with the windows when winter camping is the condensation. We've tried a number of products that are supposed to absorb the humidity, but haven't had much luck. So now, we crack open a window every night and give our four-year-old the job of drying all the windows every morning. Thanks to the snowbirds who want insulation from the heat in Florida, thermopane windows are now becoming more common in newer RVs and they not only help with the cold, but with the condensation.

Water

Since we don't use the water from our trailer in the winter, we make sure to park close to the washroom. Even still, kids will be kids and they won't always give themselves enough time to get to the washroom, especially at night, so we keep a potty on hand for emergencies. Also, our kids have accidently forgotten that we didn't have water to flush and used the toilet in the trailer. We flushed it with winterizing chemicals, so the pipes wouldn't freeze and it all came out in the spring.

At the winter campgrounds in the National Parks, parks staff often let you do your dishes in the washroom, so a dishwater pan and tray is handy for carrying your dishes to the washroom. Sometimes, I don't ask for help with the dishes, because the peaceful walk to the bathroom in the still wintery wilderness is when I soak up the moonlit snow-covered mountains and glistening stars. It is almost a spiritual moment for me.

RVers who have a winter package and who plan to hook up to the winter campground's water supply should make sure the campground's water is heated, and talk to their dealer to make sure all the hoses, holding and water tanks won't freeze.

Groups

If you are camping in a group, park near the cookhouse as well as the washroom. If you bring plastic and a staple gun or duct tape from home, you can tarp off the cookhouse windows and fire up the stove to create a cozy place to visit, cook and play games.

Clothes

Dressing properly is crucial to prevent frostbite and hypothermia and to make our time outside much more comfortable and plentiful. Loose-fitting, layers made of breathable material to wick away moisture is best. Polypropylene, wool and Gortex are good materials in really cold weather.

As soon as we crawl out from the sleeping bags in the morning, we throw on the long underwear and it stays on all day, unless the afternoon is too warm. Then depending on the weather (and the age of the kids, because of course they know best as they get older - note sarcasm), we throw fleece pants and a turtleneck on everyone. When they head outside, I have three-layer-jackets and either wind or snow pants to cover their bodies. Hats cover their heads where most of the heat can escape. The 99 cent gloves are great for road hockey games or active games like soccer and warm waterproof mittens are a necessity for playing in the snow. I bring a couple of sets of each for each child so they don't have to wait while they dry out.

Even for hiking, we wear loose-fitting, well-insulated winter boots. Leather hiking boots and thick socks will hold moisture in and your feet will get cold. One of the biggest reasons I never enjoyed winter was cold feet, but since I bought myself some good thermal socks and a pair of rather ugly, but warm winter boots, I will stay outside for hours and love it.

As the day warms up, layers come off. As it cools down, the layers go on again.

All the extra winter clothes take up space, but because we don't use our bathroom in the winter, our tub holds all our outerwear. A small tote in the tub holds all our mittens and hats.

I will admit that I was grateful the day when my youngest could get his winter wear on and off on his own. But seeing the bright red cheeks puffed around his big grin and knowing how the brisk fresh wintery air would make him sleep that night made the constant dressing and undressing worth it.

Activities

Before you leave home, check to see if there is snow on the ground at your destination or if the ski hills and skating rinks are open. Some of the towns have a webcam to show you the town at real-time, or you may want to phone. There is no point bringing toboggans, cross-country skis or showshoes if there is no snow on the ground. Mild winters have resulted in us playing a lot of road-hockey over the last few years. We have to play with two tennis balls because Sadie always tries to get the ball and when she does we play with the other ball until she gets that one.

Money we save on hotels goes towards an afternoon or two of downhill skiing on our trips. We have put our children in the daycare on a number of ski hills over the years and have been happy with all of them. Our youngest though refused to stay once his bigger sister started skiing and so he started skiing on a harness from the top of Sunshine Ski Resort in Banff at 2 1/2 years old. As with most of the youngest kids in a large family, he doesn't know that he is not supposed to be able to do the things his siblings does.

So if you have a hard-sided trailer, and the spirit for an exceptional winter camping vacation, go for it. And if you don't have a hard-sided trailer, rent one and see if it is your secret to enjoying our long Canadian winter!

Countdown to Takeoff – Packing

As any parent knows, children are programmed to interrupt you as soon as they hear you pick up the phone, turn on the computer or start packing. Also their schedules and chauffeur needs don't stop because you want to prepare for a camping trip. So, rather than stress yourself and everyone around you by trying to pack in one day, (which has been done before!) I normally divide my tasks and begin preparing for the trip three days in advance.

Remember, as kids grow older they can take on some of these tasks!!

Three days before

- I postpone the laundry until three days before we leave. I wash everything and dry everything but don't fold.

- I check to make sure my sports and craft totes aren't missing anything and the medicine bag is stocked. They get put by the door, along with a pile of empty totes.

- I decide on a menu and make a food list for that menu. This list becomes my packing and shopping list. (I might cook extra food tonight to take on the trip.)

- If I know the kids won't need their outwear (raincoats, boots, or gloves, for example,) before we go, I throw them in a bucket by the door.

- I gather all electronics, games, CD's, and walkie-talkies or nursery monitors that we plan to take and put them in a bucket. I download and clear all of the pictures from the digital camera and begin the process of recharging all the batteries. We also throw in a power converter that we can plug in our cigarette lighter and a power bar to hook up the DVD or in case someone's batteries don't work.

- I cancel newspapers, mail and milk delivery and any appointments on my calendar.

Grouch starter

I hate having to run to the trailer and bring something back in the house just to make a snack or a coffee. I have already packed it and unpacking before the trip makes me grouchy. If you are taking the last of an ingredient from in the house, consider whether you will need it before you leave or even when you get back. If you are only gone three days and you know you will go through this ingredient when you get back, leave it in the house and put it on your shopping list.

Sanity saver

When the kids were babies, I couldn't leave them alone in the house while I put away things in the trailer, so I filled buckets with all the things that needed to go out and put them by the door. I thought I was super organized but - so were the kids. They promptly unpacked when I went back to get more. It was a game to them: I pack, they unpack, I pack, they unpack . . . I killed their fun, but saved my sanity when I started to put lids on the totes. As they got wiser, I stacked the totes, and finally moved them into the garage.

Two days before

- I keep recharging batteries.

- As I fold the clothes, I pull out what we need to go camping and throw it in the "under-the-bench" buckets; one for each person. I don't want to dig for clothes, so I stack them as outfits, not pants on the bottom and shirts on top. Remember outfits might include layers. Rolling the clothes saves space.

- Each child's underwear and socks go into their own clear Ziploc bags because in the morning, when someone is sleeping on the bench, I can dress the kids in the clothes from the day before but I want clean underwear and socks easily accessible. So I pop the bags into one of the drawers under the coats in the closet. NOTE: If you have kids the same size, label the bags. If there is only one clean pair of underwear, it could be the catalyst for a simmering sibling battle.

- Bathing suits all get lumped together and put into one bag, because if we are going swimming, I can save time if I don't have to go into each person's bag or bucket. We simply grab the swimming bag and, if we go to a pool, we rent towels, especially in the winter when it is difficult to find a warm place to hang six big towels while they dry. Also, we don't need to use up space with big bulky beach towels unless we are at a lake or beach.

- AS SOON AS THE RV COMES HOME from storage (which is often two days before we leave) I immediately plug in the power and turn on the fridge. If it is winter, I also plug in the electric heater with fan, so I can pack food, clothes and unload groceries without freezing.

- Then I take stock of what needs to be replenished in the trailer. They are things like sugar, pet food, soap, towels, paper towels, garbage bags. If I have extras in the house, I put them in one of the buckets going to the trailer. If I need to buy them, they go on my food/shopping list.

- I put all the contents of the buckets in the trailer in their proper place.

- On a good day, when my husband came home, I would leave the kids with him and find peace and quiet in the warm trailer while I unpacked. Needless to say, I would take my time and enjoy the serenity. There were some times though when I had to bring at least one child into the trailer with me while I unpacked. I just put them at the table with blocks.

- Either I or the kids fill their car bag and I recheck and refill the baby's bribery bag (see bribery and car bags pg. 60.) I add their surprise toy for the trip and put it by the door. (If I think they will go into it, I put it on the bench in the trailer.)

Warning!

If it is winter and you are loading the trailer, make sure the electric heater is plugged in and the furnace is turned on as a backup. If something goes wrong and your trailer gets cold, any liquids (except the alcohol) will freeze and possible explode!!

One day before

- Go through the food list and fill the buckets with food. Remember not to take the last bit of an item (see Grouchstarter above). The trailer's fridge should be cold, so you can put the fridge items in. Remember, since you are putting the smaller containers of condiments that you filled in the trailer, you will still have the ketchup and butter for meals until you leave. Scratch the food off the list as it goes into the trailer. If you have something that you don't want to bring into the trailer yet, put a check mark beside it so you don't buy it when grocery shopping.

- Take the grocery list, as well as any other lists of things to buy and go shopping.

- Remember something small for the bribery bags! When you come back from shopping, if there is fresh fruit or vegetables, rinse them, and put them into the trailer. Unload everything else directly into the trailer.

- Save time by creating a bucket for everything that goes in the car (car box) and put it by the door. (See Car Box List and Surviving the road trip). This will include travelling snacks, wet wipes, extra garbage bags, a few Ziploc bags and if there are babies, a restocked diaper bag with at least one extra bottle to pour juice or water into.

- There will also be food that you need to prepare just before your trip, but you don't want to forget to put in the trailer. Here is a strategy to ensure you remember. If you are making coffee, hot chocolate and bagels for the trip in the morning, leave the refrigerated ingredients like milk, cream cheese and jam together in a bag in the fridge. Leave non-refrigerated food like coffee and bagels in a bag on a clean counter, with the travel mugs and bottles that you will need for the trip.

- Wash any last-minute clothes, throw them in the appropriate bucket and put them in the trailer. If you couldn't put the outerwear in before, load them now.

- Double check if all the electronics are still in the box (mine tend to disappear), load the ones that go in the trailer, and put the ones that go in the car in the car box. Remember the power converter, power bar and speakers if you are playing a movie on your portable DVD player in the car.

- Load any remaining filled buckets/boxes into the trailer, except the car box.

- Fill the water jug.

- If you are travelling in the morning, ensure that as many of the things that you'll need to load in the hours just before you leave (see section below) are ready by the door.

Car bags and Bribery bags:

Bribery bags are little backpacks that I fill to entertain the young children or babies. It might include stuffies, rattles, little cars, small books, and teethers. Their attention span is short, so you will need more books or toys for them than for an older child. I let the kids fill their own car bags. They get one backpack to take in the car and as they get older they decide what goes into it. I suggest sketch paper, pencil crayons or pencil with pencil sharpener, activity books, books, favorite toys (not too small or they will get lost in the car) and their own electronics.

For bribery and car bags, I put a surprise toy in, either something new or something odd that will be a conversation starter or that can be used in a game.

Hours before you leave

- Set timers on lamps, small pet feeding systems, and adjust timers on thermostat

- Before anyone gets anything in the car, I put towels on the seats and bench to catch food or pencils or toys. The towels can also do double duty, to help someone clean up if they get sick.

- If you have a travel trailer and not a motorhome, load the car with a coat or shoes for each child in case you need to stop.

- Load the bribery bags and car bags, if the kids haven't loaded them already.

- Pull the bag of ingredients out of the fridge and use the bag on the counter (see CAR FOOD one day before) to make the bagels, the coffee and hot chocolate (or whatever you are having) and put all ingredients back into the bag. Both bags go out to the trailer.

- The only thing left on the counter should be the snacks and drinks that go into the car. Put them with the car food container and load it. Hopefully the car food container can fit at the front seat passenger's feet, ready for you to administer. If not, try to find a spot within reach of you, but not within reach of the kids.

Much of what you do at this point depends on when you leave. We prefer to travel in the evening or early morning with our kids, so they sleep.

Early Risers – If we leave in the morning,

- I start the coffee and prepare the bagels and then load those ingredients, the car box and anything else that was by the door in the car or trailer, including the food bag and coffee.

- I wake the kids, and then while they go to the washroom, I build their nests in the car with their pillows and blanket and throw their car and bribery bags in. They jump in and go back to sleep. When they wakeup, they can dig into their bags until we stop for gas or breakfast and send them in the trailer to get dressed.

Evening trips – For evening trips,

- I throw the car box and anything else that was by the door in the car or trailer, including the ingredients that I left out to make drinks or snacks to be eaten in the car.

- Then the kids or I build their nests and bring in their car and bribery bags. If it is dark or it will be a long trip, I set up the DVD player or TV.

- We send the kids to the bathroom and put the kids in the car wearing their pajamas and if need be, fresh diapers, or pull-ups. We start a movie and I let them fall asleep.

Minutes before you leave

Do one last walk through your house and lock the doors. Check that everything is stored securely in your trailer.

Check that the water pump is off.

Check that all doors and windows on the trailer are closed and locked. Check that the vents and antennas are down and check that the step is in.

COUNT YOUR KIDS!

Surviving the Road Trip

et's face it, road trips are sometimes meant to reinforce the benefits of birth control. Between the kids fighting, getting carsick and having to stop for the bathroom, getting to the campground can make childbirth sound easy. We have some strategies that might help.

Best time for travelling

If we can help it, we travel either early, early morning or we leave in the evening and travel late at night. That way the kids sleep most of the way so we can have quiet, private time and we don't have to stop as often. If we travel in the morning, we pack the night before, and morning or night, we put the kids in the car in their pajamas.

Avoid pit stops

No drinks right before we leave and of course, we send them all to the bathroom just before we leave.

Drink patrol

Minimize the drinks in the car and have caps or lids to seal them when they are not in use. Wise parents only give their kids water in the car. We sometimes give our kids juices or non-sugar drinks but we definitely draw the line at caffeine drinks (for the kids at least). I keep all drinks with me until they are an age when I know they won't guzzle them quickly and they can control their bladder. I pass them their drink for the occasional swig, and ask for it after they are finished drinking to put the cap on properly. If it is evening, and we know the little one needs a bottle in the car to sleep, we put a pull-up on him/her.

Exploding sippy cups

Never put pop in a sippy cup when travelling. The bumps get the carbon dioxide going and the resulting pressure will redecorate the ceiling in your car.

Wise snacking

Snacks shouldn't be salty, or the kids will be thirsty and drink too much. They shouldn't be too sweet or they will be bouncing off the car doors before the trip is half done. Though I love to bring fruit, berries have been dropped and stepped on, leaving stains. Grapes are good, but make sure you peel them, bite them or cut them, for the little ones; whatever it takes to make sure they won't choke. Fish crackers or the mini crackers with peanut butter or cheeze whiz in them are good. My kids like sausage or pepperoni sticks and cheese. I cut it up as we travel so it is fresh. Bagels and cream cheese are another alternative, especially in the morning. As we get closer to our destination, the good stuff comes out. Maybe liquorice or chips. And of course, we have smarties for the smartie game close to the end of the trip. (see travel games below)

Prime nesting sites

Decide who sits in the prime seats before the trip, and let the others know they have first dibs for the prime seats on the way back. You might want to determine this by who helped most with the packing! We let each child take one pillow and one blanket along with one backpack or carbag to create their nest.

Electronic saviours

Bring speakers and headphones if you are planning on allowing electronics on the trip. (Earplugs are another option.) For long evening trips we usually rent a couple of family movies that no one has seen before, but everyone has to agree on the movie or music (and of course it has to be appropriate for all) if a movie or CD will be played out loud.

Kids travelling games

If the electronics are off, and the kids are tired of reading, drawing or coloring, we play games. In one we use the letters of license plates and challenge them to think of a word or a silly phrase. For example, we might make PCS into Purple Crocodile Snot. Of course, the more body fluids, the more giggles. Another distraction is to ask the kids what they see in the clouds. You can also grow a "fortunate-unfortunate" story with each person adding a sentence changing the story from a fortunate to an unfortunate and back to a fortunate situation. Math skills can improve with a "Buzz" game, where everyone takes turns saying numbers but if a number is divisible by 5, the person has to say buzz. (There are some great ideas for travelling games on Momsminivan.com.) If you are in a motor home you can buckle the kids at the table and play magnetic travel games that won't slide around if you hit a bump. Singing and finger rhymes also help the time pass.

Smartie game

About a half-hour before the end of the trip, when the "when are we going to be there?" questions are becoming unbearable, we start the smartie game. We think of questions for each child focusing on something they have recently learned about, or for the young ones, their name, phone number, address, or emergency number. If they get it right they get one smartie. If you are too tired to think of questions, use math or spelling or use trivia cards from board games.

Quiet game

Need a break? This game is the best. Challenge everyone to see who can be the quietest and stillest for the longest.

Baby's games

If you are travelling with a baby, check out the RVing with Babies to Preschoolers' chapter for travelling tips

Surprise object

I pack something special in the bottom of every child's car bag, or baby's bribery bag. It can be used as a distraction when they start picking at each other. It might be a book, a game, a craft, or something really odd, like an egg cup or a baby spoon. Then you can play a game where you think of as many uses as possible for it. Slip a piece of aluminum foil or pipe cleaners into their backpack and let them use their imagination to create something with them. Also finger puppets don't take much space and can create hours of fun.

Entering the Campground

Congratulations! You have survived the road trip and arrived at the campground. If you have reserved they will have a site pre-booked for you. Though we try to specify in our reservation request where we want to be, if they put us in another site, we usually ask a few questions about the site to see if it will work with our trailer and our kids.

- Will our trailer fit? Imagine your trailer in the spot with your awning open. Would the firepit be right under the awning? Would trees block you from your storage areas? Are you likely to lose a mirror backing up?

- Is it a drive-through spot ? This is important if the driver isn't comfortable backing up. NOTE: Navigating the backup has been known to cause divorces. You may want to practice hand signals before you go.

- Are there any cliffs? How close to the river is it? Depending on how deep and fast the river is and the age of the kids, you don't want to be too close.

- Is there a shallow stream nearby? This can provide hours of enjoyment for kids.

- Is it a treed spot? Some trees are nice for shade, but take a look. If the branches are too low, you can lose sight of the kids easily. You may also want some open space for the kids to run.

- Is there a playground nearby?

- If you want to conserve water in your trailer, or if you have seniors who have trouble walking, are you close to the washroom?

- Check to see who your neighbours are. You can't always judge a book by its cover because they may be annoying or leave the next day, but having kids nearby can be a benefit especially if you have only one child. If your neighbors are six young beer drinkers with music blaring in the middle of the afternoon, I would request another site.

NOTE: Even though you are assigned a spot, you can always ask for a different spot. If you aren't satisfied with the spot they gave you, drive around. Get out and explore. If you find the perfect site and it looks empty, check the site marker to see if it has a tag with a date. If not, or if the date has expired, leave someone or something there and go back to the gate to see if you can move. If it is open and not booked they will usually switch you.

RV Etiquette

Rule #1

Don't take someone else's spot. Sometimes, people in a motor home will go on a daytrip and not leave anything at the site or they just leave a chair, or something on the table. If there is something left, they are probably coming back. There might also be a stub with the check-out date attached to the site marker. If you still want to know for sure, check at the entrance or with parks staff to see if the spot is free.

Rule #2

Especially in the Rocky Mountains, but wherever there are wild animals, always clean everything up and put all food equipment in a vehicle when you go away from your site. Garbage or food that is left out attracts animals, and if they become bothersome, they have to be moved or put down. In the Rocky Mountains and some other locations, parks staff will remove any stoves or food left out and you have to go collect them when you return.

Rule #3

Grey water, should only be dumped where indicated by the campground. Grey water and sewage coming directly from the trailer goes into the dump station. If you have some left-over coffee that for one reason or another you don't want to drop into your system, read the signs in the washrooms. They sometimes suggest you pour grey water in the toilets in the public washrooms, in dishwashing sinks attached to the outside of the washroom, or at the water taps outside. Pouring it in the bush next to your camper attracts animals.

Rule #4

Be considerate and respectful of neighbours. Don't cut through other people's sites if at all possible. If you are using the public washrooms and showers, please be quick if there is a lineup and clean up afterwards. Respect quiet hours and the hours for charging your generator and don't play your music too loud. We don't worry if our kids are loud when they are playing and laughing during the day, but if they start fighting or screaming, we ask them to be quiet or put them inside the trailer or the car. We don't want to hear fights, and assume our neighbours don't want to as well.

Rule #5

If you have a barking dog, make him be quiet or put him in the truck or trailer. Also, tie pets up, preferably to your trailer, a picnic table or stake, so you don't damage the bark on a tree. Tying your pet up may be as important to your neighbours as it is to your dogs' well-being. Neighbours want to enjoy the serenity and may not want a dog roaming through their campsite. As for your dogs' well-being, he or she may run after wild animals and get hurt. Just because you are in the wilderness, doesn't mean you don't have to pick up the doggie doos. Campsites are places where kids play and they shouldn't have to step in it.

Rule #6

We don't let our kids go into other people's trailers. We encourage them to play in a play tent or at the picnic table if they want to play a board game. That is our basic rule, however, if we get to know the parents and are feeling comfortable, they may be able to go in but we want to be able to see them through the window when we walk by.

Rule #7

Make sure the fire is out, before you retire for the evening and before you leave the campsite.

Rule #8

Always leave no trace. Put trash away, recycle where possible, and don't leave trash in the firepit for the next camper. Leave the site, dump station and showers or washroom as clean as when you came.

If you set up clotheslines, or stapled or taped plastic in the cookhouse windows and doors, take everything home, right down to the staples and/or tape.

Coming Home

t has been a great trip and you pushed it to the very last minute. It is almost 10 p.m. when you pull in to your driveway and your kids have school and you have work the next day. You're relaxed and you don't want to unpack the whole trailer before you retire. You are just looking forward to a hot shower and sleeping in your own bed.

Since you're probably too tired to think, I've made a list of what you have to do before you go to sleep, so you can get to work and school the next day.

Things to bring inside

- Your kids! Along with their nesting blankets, and pillows.
- Electronics from in the car.
- Grooming kits
- Medicine
- One tub of food -include milk and breakfast items and the ingredients you need if you have to pack lunches
- One set of clothes and outerwear per person for the next day.

(If you know you have enough of these items left in the house for one day, skip the last two items.)

Things to do before you sleep

- Plug in your trailer and turn on the fridge.
- Turn on the heater (and furnace for backup) if it is below freezing outside.
- Unhook your truck if you need it the next morning.
- If the clothes or outerwear smell smoky and you need them for school or work the next day, throw them immediately into the washer!
- NOW, go have your shower and enjoy your own bed like you have never enjoyed it before! Tomorrow, the kids can help unload. . .

Journal on the drive home!

I always write in my journal on our way home from our holiday, while everything is fresh. I ask our family to reflect and share what they thought were the best and the worst parts of the trip and when they laughed the hardest on our trip.

I include these memories along with who we camped with, who we met, what we did and where we went.

If you include the facts like the dates, destination, weather and whether we reserved or not it makes it quite interesting to look back in the years to come.

One final item I always include is information about our campsite and any preferred campsite numbers, so when we reserve next time, we can get the best spot for us.

RVing with Babies to Preschoolers

What better way to bond with a new baby than to remove yourself from all distractions so you can focus on him or her. A healthy newborn's world revolves around their Mom, Dad and siblings. They revel in the secure feeling of being surrounded by the ones they love.

On a warm summer day when you are RVing, you will spend most of your time outside, relaxing with your baby and breathing in the fresh air. There is no phone, visitors, or housework. You can nap when you want and if you are nursing, even better! You hardly need to bring anything with you!

My son should not have even been born when we took him on his first camping trip. He was seven weeks premature, but we went camping with him when he was six weeks old. We were in a tent trailer at that time, and I still think it was one of the best things we could have done. The fresh air was just what he needed to sleep longer and longer. He quickly learned to sleep wherever he was which made him much more flexible for our busy life. And away from home, I couldn't do anything but relax when he was sleeping.

Taking a baby RVing can range from no work at all to a lot of work depending at which stage they are. Nursing newborns are the easiest. No bottles to wash and the fresh air tires them out. Of course Dad will have to pitch in with the packing of the trailer, (nothing like Mom's recent labour) but once you are out there, depending on the age of the infant, it can be easy or challenging. A toddler who has just discovered the freedom of travelling on his own motor power can be quite a bit more challenging. Here are some tips we found helped.

Use baby's schedule

Whether you are the type of parent who keeps a strict routine or not, try to plan around your baby's normal schedule. You can be more flexible with your own schedule especially when camping.

Remember KISS

That's Keep It Small for Space. You don't want to bring the whole house when you RV but babies can take a lot of equipment. Find equipment that is compact; inflatable travel beds, umbrella strollers, fold up play pens. Try to find things that can do double duty. Let your toddler push the umbrella stroller with her baby, instead of bringing a doll stroller.

Travelling time tips

Games for babies

Some children travel well and some don't. I was lucky. My kids did, but my trick was to keep them entertained until they fell asleep. I used the bribery bag and we would play finger games, peek-a-boo and sing songs.

Diaper bag

Include at least one extra empty bottle in your diaper bag. If they start the trip with a bottle of milk, of course they will want a bottle of juice and you will soon master pouring the juice from the juice box into a bottle without having to stop the RV.

Bribery bag

Keep a bribery pack close at hand with drinks, snacks, toys, books and something special that she/he hasn't seen before. (See sidebar in 'Countdown to Takeoff' chapter.)

Drop-stoppers

Pin the soother to the child and attach one end of a leash on the bottle and the other on the baby's chair or seatbelt, so you don't have to crawl in the back every time he drops his bottle. I made my leashes out of those colourful connecting rings. They are safer than a nylon cord, more fun, he can chew on them when he is teething, and you can attach his favorite toy to it as well. Travelling close to nap time is a good plan, if you can.

Feeding baby

Emergency soothers

If you use soothers, make sure you have a few extra in a sterile ziploc bag in case they get lost. Also, bring a lot of bibs. It saves changing clothes.

Nursing moms

If you drink lots of fluids and eat healthy, the relaxed setting and lifestyle of RVing, should help your body make more milk. Besides, you will have the time to enjoy nursing your baby with no pressures or schedules. If you are needing to pump milk for some reason, and your RV has a freezer in it, line your bottle with bottle liners first. When you are done pumping, remove the liner and freeze the milk in the liner. Leave enough space for it to expand.

Food equipment

Bottle feeders need a day-and-a-half supply of bottles, nipples and lids (kept in a sterile zip loc bag), bottle liners, powdered formula, thermos (good size), large pot to boil water and sterilize nipples, and a sterile water bottle.

Nursing Moms need nothing, unless they need to pump. Then, along with the pump, they can use the same equipment as the bottle feeders, with the exception of the formula and water bottle.

Reduce work

If you use liners so you don't have to wash bottles, and if you bring enough nipples, you may only have to sterilize the nipples once a day. Boil one big pot of water. Fill a thermos and a water bottle. Then sterilize nipples in the remaining water. Store sterile nipples in a zip-loc bag.

When he needs it NOW!

When you need to feed your baby NOW, put the powder formula in a bottle liner and add hot water from the thermos until 1/3 full. Add the cold sterilized water from the water bottle to cool it so it is not too hot to drink.

If nursing and using frozen pumped milk, you can quickly warm it in a mug of hot water from the thermos. Always try to have one liner of milk thawed in the fridge for quick use.

Troubleshooting

If the bottles and nipples you use don't work with disposable bottle liners, try to insert the liner into your bottle anyways.

If you do it up tight, you can make it work. It really helps reduce the work load.

As he/she grows

The double-duty thermos also comes in handy for sterilized water or hot milk when the child grows out of formula and needs cereals. After that, I take the easy way and buy jars of food for camping. If you are one of those supermoms who prepares homemade baby food, more power to you! You can bring your food cubes along in the freezer and warm them with the hot water from the thermos.

Challenge #1: Family Dinner Time

Taking care of baby when you are trying to get his/her dinner ready or the family's dinner on or off the table will probably be one of the most challenging times of your day. This is especially true while they are growing into the toddler stage, or if you have other small children. They are hungry and so are you.

Avoid pre-meal meltdowns

Feed them first, so you can enjoy your meal.

Safety during meal prep

To keep them safe while preparing the meal, put them in a playpen, if they will go into one. Our baby hated it, so my husband and I would take turns cooking and getting dinner on the table, while the other parent watched the little ones, or we'd put the baby in a snugli, and multi-task.

As they grow

Once they could sit up, we would throw them into our baby carrier/backpack, so they could watch us over our shoulder, They also like to sit at the table like the big people, but booster chairs would fall off the bench, or would sit too far back from the table and food would fall everywhere. So bring out a dinner chair (with a safety buckle) that attachs to the top of the picnic or RV table right next to where you are and put toys in front of him.

Catch-all rug

Throw down a straw mat or table cloth underneath the table so toys don't get full of dirt if he drops them. It is also a fast and easy way to clean up dropped food so you don't attract animals after dinner.

Challenge #2: Blowouts

Protect the sleeping bag

I usually bring double what I need when it comes to diapers and sleepers. You can use biodegradable disposable diapers, which helps the environment. But sometimes, even disposable diapers are not enough and the mess goes up the back, down the legs in the sleepers, and even on the sleeping bag. I do recommend sleepers because, along with keeping the baby warm, it does trap much of the mess and stops it from ending up on the sleeping bag. I also recommend getting the waterproof mattress pads they use in hospitals, with the plastic inside the material. It protects the sleeping bags and trailer cushions from getting wet or soiled. I bring three and if they all get soiled, I wash them under a tap, in a creek or if I need to escape before the next dump happens, I make a trip into town to the nearest Laundromat.

Cleaning up

To clean up, a huge tub of disposable wet ones will do the job. You need to have a lot of washcloths with you, but for messy stools, use paper towels or disposable wet ones, to wipe most of it off. They can be put in a bag and thrown in the garbage. Hopefully, then, you will only need one washcloth per blowout. Most RV's have a hand-held shower head which can be used, and for those that aren't, there should be showers in the campground. Dirty clothes can be taken to the tap in the campground or to a river or creek and washed out, at least enough so it doesn't stink. Make sure you let the clothes dry before putting them in your dirty laundry bag, or your laundry will grow mould before you get home.

Potty-training

Don't give up on potty-training just because you are camping. We would bring a potty and leave it outside of the trailer. Getting in the trailer to the washroom, sometimes takes too long. If you are concerned about nighttime, pull-ups are another option.

Sleeping

Primitive travel beds

When our babies were little, we didn't do the research on babies' travel beds. We just put rolled up towels on each side of our babies, so they couldn't roll around. As they got bigger, duffel bags lined the edge of the bed, so they couldn't roll out of bed and our toddlers used their bed rails from home. They worked fine.

Modern travel beds

Now, there are many choices. Some travel beds are compact. They have sides that pop up and they fit on the end of a single bed. Some look like a little pup tent and double as a playpen for outdoor play during the day. They are rainproof, windproof and UV proof. Some are air mattresses with taller compartments on the side to keep babies from rolling off. You choose!

Activities

Snuggle and rest

If you are on a recoup mission, you may just want to rest by your RV. A newborn who doesn't move around much is fine in his car seat, on a blanket, or snuggling in your arms. He or she will get lots of gentle stimulation: the birds, the green trees with their rustling leaves waving against the blue sky, the gurgling of a creek if you are near one. If you have a treed site, an inexpensive hammock can be a wonderful place to snuggle with your baby. Get help getting in and out though!

Gentle walks

For relaxing walks, a snugli or a stroller is best. Don't put your newborn baby in a backpack until they are 5-6 months, and his or her neck is strong enough. Some women prefer a sling. I found if I used a sling for longer walks my back would get sore. I preferred the snugli for walks.

Strollers

A stroller is nice for walks too. We used an umbrella stroller and modified it to support our very young baby's head while we pushed it. It packed well and fit in the public washrooms when I needed to use the facilities. I also brought the baby when I showered in the campground's showers and I used public showers often to conserve water in our trailer, so it was important to have a stroller that would fit in the cubicle.

X-country strollers

In most campsites the roads are not paved, but are fairly well packed. With only a little struggle we could walk around with the umbrella stroller, but if you are planning on running with baby, or going cross country, or down trails, pick a sturdier stroller with a wider base and larger wheels. Unfortunately, they take up more space.

Double-duty strollers

If you are shopping for equipment for your baby, take a look at the new double-duty transportation options: carbed/strollers, stroller/backpacks, and carbed/playpens are some of your choices. Consider how you camp and if you have other children that will eventually use it when buying these items.

Jolly jumpers

As our kids began to stand, we brought the older space-saving jolly jumpers and tied them to trees to give our babies some exercise and entertainment. Make sure you pick a good tree branch and that it is securely tied not too close to the trunk!!

Insect protection

Since babies shouldn't use mosquito repellant with DEET, here are some alternatives. We used netting on their playpens, strollers, or car-seat/chair. We would also light a citronella candle or a mosquito-repellant coil nearby (not near toddlers, though). Light-colored long-sleeved shirts and long pants helped, and we tried some oils from the health-food store and Avon that are safe for babies and have helped.

Toddlers to Preschoolers

Safe areas for toddlers

An infant who is starting to get around is a lot trickier to take camping. You need to have holding pens or safe areas or you have to be prepared for dirt. If your child is used to a playpen, there are many portable ones that fold up easily. Ours had a lid on it to keep the sun out. Unfortunately, our child was not used to it, and so grudgingly stayed in it only while we were putting dinner on the table. We didn't set up a play tent until the babies were older because we wanted to be able to see them. During play time we would throw a mat down on the ground and put the toys on it. Of course, the dirt looks greener on the other side so she would wander and we would follow. She would crawl or walk to feel the grass, let sand run through her fingers, touch the rough bark. She was filthy but her senses would get a workout and she would be tired by nap time. Thank goodness the crawling only lasted one season.

First season of first steps

When they are first learning to walk, they want to practice and practice and practice and explore. Remind yourself that it only takes a few short months to learn how to walk.

Back saving ideas

Invest in a good push toy that doesn't tip easy when your child starts walking and give your back a break. As they get older, tricycles with push arms are a great way to save your back, because if the road is paved in front of your trailer, your preschooler will want to do the loop again and again and again.

Small safety tips

The child's first taste of freedom gives parents more to worry about. Put a bearbell on the kids at all times, not so much for the bears - it probably wouldn't scare them anyway, but so you can find them if, in the second it takes to put another log on the fire, they wander behind the trailer, or truck. We bought light-up shoes for our smaller kids, so when it got dark earlier outside in the spring and fall, we could still find them.

Safety at dinner time

There are ideas in the Family Dinner Time portion of this chapter for keeping them safe during preparation and clean-up.

KISS games

Your trailer is probably already full with camping equipment for your young family. Here are some ideas for activities with little ones that follow the Keep It Small for Space principle:

- Bring a finger play rhyme book. We would spend hours with them on our lap, learning the rhymes with the finger movements.

- Let the kids use the rings from a ring toss game as a steering wheel and they can pretend they are driving all over the campsite.

- Tie string and a piece of flat bark onto a stick and encourage the kids to pull their "pretend boat" through the water as they walk up and down the side of the creek,

- Tie a rope between two trees at the child's chest level and tie balloons on them. Let them punch or karate kick the balloons and try to turn them over the rope.

- Ask the kids to take their dolls or stuffies for a walk with the stroller. The stroller helps their balance and it keeps them busy.

- Blow bubbles for your kids. They will try to catch the dancing bubbles as they float on the wind, usually just out of reach of their fingertips. As they grow, let them try to blow the bubbles.

- My kids also loved to play with balls. Play catch with a velcro pad and tennis ball to help little people develop eye-hand coordination. Bring beach balls or punch balls which can travel without air in them.

- Modify hot wheels by bringing a few of pieces of hot wheels tracks and putting one end on the picnic table bench. Weave two sets of tracks over a couple of logs to the ground. Grab the cars and take turns racing.

- Invite older toddlers to join in on a family bocce game. You might want to use the novice bocce balls which are lighter.

- Bring nets and try to catch butterflies or insects. Bring buckets and catch water bugs or tiny fish. For your preschooler, there are small fishing rods that have plastic fish weights at the end. It is a safe way to teach your pre-schooler to cast a line, while you are fishing.

- Find rocks and a pond and you've found the perfect place to teach your kids to throw and quietly watch the ripples spread.

RVing with Children

Last year, it took 45 minutes from when the bell signalling the beginning of the summer holidays rang, for the "I'm bored" and "There's nothing to do" mantra to drag out of my kids' mouths. We rarely hear this when we are camping but if we do we are ready. Since kids have different interests, and since RVing is a chance to introduce new activities to kids, I have listed a number of activities which meet the KISS requirements and can keep the kids busy for hours.

Chores!

The standard response to the "I'm bored" mantra in our house is a list of chores that haven't been done. Though they scoff at our response, we know that when kids are involved or feeling like they are contributing, they can feel good about themselves. So kids doing chores is non-negotiable when we are camping, but we give them a few chores that they find fun. Getting the wood, setting up a playtent or fort and building a fire are chores our kids willingly do. The 'Cooking and Menu Tips' chapter has more ideas for how they can get involved at mealtime.

Activities to stimulate science senses

- catching insects, bugs, water animals (You'll need nets and Ziploc containers with holes poked in or bug houses. Sand buckets are good to catch water animals.)
- identifying flowers, trees, birds, animals, insects, bugs. (Keep reference books inside the trailer.)
- building forts, teepees (Use materials around your campsite and a tarp, blankets and bungee cords.)
- building bows and arrows or slingshots (Use bendable branches and string or elastic.)
- collecting shells, fossils, petrified wood
- finding animal homes
- identifying habitats
- damming creeks or streams
- fishing
- making bubbles

Sports kids

- soccer, baseball, volleyball, football, beachball
- skipping
- biking
- hiking and rock jumping or rock climbing
- fording streams
- rock skipping
- snow board surfing
  We tie a rope between two trees and in the middle of that rope, we tie a rope which hangs down and attaches to one end of a 3-foot piece of wood. That end should be 6" off the ground. Then the kids balance on the piece of wood while hanging on to the rope in front of them.

- balloon kicking and punching
  A rope between two trees and a couple of balloons can create hours of fun. We set the rope at the kids' waist level and tie a balloon to it (punch balloons work best). Then they can kick it or punch it and the object is to make it spin around the rope.
- badminton and frisbee (Only do this if there is no wind or you have a fairly large open space.)
- road hockey
- bocce (great even for toddlers!)
- water gun fights (great activity for a hot day!)
- hopscotch
- night tag (with flashlights and within boundaries)
- roller blading, skateboards and scooters (First check to see if campground roads are paved.)

Winter

- skiing
- skating/hockey
- road hockey
- cross-country skiing
- tobogganing
- building forts with snow
- making snow caves
- snowball fights
- snowshoeing
- dog-sledding
- skijoring

Craft kids

- whittling (if the kids are old enough)
- building boats to sail on a stream
- rock painting (Find unusual rocks and paint them into ladybugs or other animals with outdoor craft paint. Seal the finished product with varnish or flour and water)
- corn husk dolls
- drawing, painting
- chalk drawing (Perfect activity if the road in the campsite is paved. Try hopscotch or X's and O's or draw a welcome sign from your family.)
- building sand castles
- decorating the fort
- playing with play dough. It can be used like a glue to hold rocks together or attach pipe cleaners to rocks, or to make different things.
- pipe cleaner creations

- building homes or space ships from paper plates or plastic cups, or blocks
- tin foil creations
- foam sticker creations
- making friendship bracelets or bead jewellery
- sand art (You can make pictures on construction paper by gluing sand in certain places. You can even color the sand by rubbing chalk on it.)
- make a mobile by gluing or tying pine cones, shells or other natural objects to twigs.

Cooking kids

Cooking over the fire – Most kids love a fire and the idea of cooking whole meals over a fire, makes them want to get involved - especially if it involves sweet desserts and snacks. When our kids were young we started by getting them to prepare smores, banana splits and pies or turnovers for cooking over the fire. As they got older, they prepared their own pizzas and bannock. Now they can make their own foil pocket for dinner. Kids often think outside of the box and after rummaging in the cupboard, come up with some creative meals.

Kids' Café – When the kids' grandmother joins us for camping she sets up "Oma's Café" every morning. As soon as we wake up, we wander to Oma's café (her trailer) and she has our coffee, hot chocolate and homemade muffins ready. The kids wanted to return the favor and created the Kids' Café which they open occasionally in the afternoon. They cut up oranges (with my help), dip them in lemon juice and sprinkle sugar on them for a tasty, fresh snack. They make some interesting creations with their mini-marshmallows and toothpicks for an edible centrepiece. They also share treats from the treat cupboard.

Creative kids

- **Operate a restaurant** - Young entrepreneurial spirits can set up stores using pine cones or pebbles as currency, cook imaginary dishes to sell like pine needle stew, or green leaf souffle and make menus and signs for their restaurant.

- **Paper Maché** - A family I met brings flour and makes a paper mache pinata the day they arrive. It is messy, so they make it and paint it before they go for showers or to the lake. The pinata hangs in their campsite until the day before they leave when they break it and share the treats.

- **Marshmallows and toothpicks** - From molecules to airplanes, this edible craft can be made into all types of things. Don't do this too close to dinner!

- **Cowboys and Indians** - Use the sling shots and bows made from branches and string. We get our kids to use only pine cones and straws as weapons -no rocks or pointed sticks.

- **Boat building** - If you are near a stream, try to build a number of different types of boats and see which ones float best.

- **Mobile making** - Make a mobile with sticks, string and pine cones, or with sea shells. You are only limited by your imagination.

- **Write** - Have kids who love to write fill in the RVers journal

- **Capture the holiday** - Give a child a camera and make

him or her the official photographer. Then have them scrapbook pictures and souvenirs from the trip.

- **Future Filmmakers** - Encourage your youngsters film-making skills by letting them videotape special moments on your trip

Campfire activities

My kids love to sit by the campfire because we always try to make it fun for them. They always get included in the conversations and activities, whether it is playing games or taste testing experimental treats.

Ghost Stories – Old standard camp-fire ghost stories are always a hit, but we give them funny endings rather than scary ones until they are older, or until the younger ones have gone to bed. My older kids have taken to reading them during the year, so they have new ghost stories to tell when camping.

Minus-the-Board Games – When we sit around the fire, we modify board games and play without the board. For example, we just ask Disney trivia questions, and may or may not keep score depending on the mood of the kids.

Playing with words – We also play some of our travelling games (see 'Surviving the Road Trip' chapter). For example, we makeup stories with everyone adding a line to a story, or we go around the circle, coming up with an animal or food for each letter of the alphabet.

Interpretive Programs – Some campgrounds host very informative and entertaining nature programs in the summer. Often one of us takes the kids while the other does the dishes and lights the fire. The kids try to remember as much as they can about what they learned and then try to educate the other parent around the campfire.

Outdoor night time activities

Because we camp during all four seasons our kids have often been awake when darkness sets in. As the nights get longer, 7 p.m. is too early to start the bedtime routine, though it is already dark. We have found some wonderful ways to keep our eyes on them, while we relax by the camp-fire and let them still be active in the campground.

Light up the night – We bring along one long stringy glow-stick per person. After dark they do a show for us, swinging it around and making patterns with it. Then they wear it around their neck or wrist so we can see them when they walk away from the campfire. We have played hide and seek in a dark open field and when they are young enough they don't realize that you can see them because of their necklaces. Shoes that light up are also great to keep track of little ones at night. Of course, make sure they don't get out of hearing range in case you lose sight of them.

Stargazing – Because campgrounds are typically dark, they are great places to see the stars. When my daughter took astronomy in Grade 6 Science, we purchased a telescope and all learned to identify the solar systems. On a clear night in the middle of winter, we invade and heat up the public cookhouse and set up the telescope in the door.

"Head" off the night – If the kids want to bike or have a game of bocce or continue a board game in the dark, we occasionally pull out the headlamps as a special treat. Of course, if the kids are biking, rules like not leaving the road are set to stop them from running into trees.

Indoor night time activities

Rainy nights or cold winter nights shouldn't be wasted just because you can't be outside. You can move into a cookhouse if it is raining, especially if you are in a big group. Waterproof play tents can be a fun place for a kid's board game. If we are alone, we will sometimes take the kids to the nearest town's swimming pool, bowling alley or movie theatre. A quiet night playing games, reading, crafts or watching a movie in the trailer might be just what we need, too.

Games

- Board Games
- Card games
- Dice games
- Puzzles
- Treasure Hunts

Get their input

We usually end the night by asking the kids what their favorite activity was that day and share our plans for the next day.

A place of their own

As the kids grow, they want more independence and privacy. (And SO DO WE!!!) We usually set up a play tent where they can play board games, or tell ghost stories if they don't feel like joining us around the campfire. Sometimes they would go there for some quiet time or with their Game Boys. If they meet friends at the campground, they often retreat in the tent to play cards or to set up a play area for their Pet Shop pets or Polly Pockets (both small toys).

Opportunity to reset sleep patterns

RVing provides a great opportunity to reset kids' sleeping patterns easily whenever bedtimes get out of control. We always do this on the September long weekend, when we have to prepare our kids for early school mornings. After staying up late all summer, kids don't want to go to bed early and, at home, they are very aware of what time it is. When RVing, our sense of time disappears and hunger builds quickly, so it is easy to shift dinner earlier and make the kids ready for bed earlier. They still get fireside time because it is dark earlier in the fall and after a full day outdoors, they are tired. (Maybe we are bad parents, but once our kids could read a clock, we either hid it, or turned it back an hour!)

Taking teens camping

There comes a time when kids grow up and their friends and making money becomes more important than camping with their family. It's understandable, and part of you will want to let them stay home or with friends to avoid the battles and hormonal upheavals typical of the teen years.

We actually like having our daughter with us. We need a bigger trailer and I would like an escape hatch sometimes, but we know she needs to get away from the politics of school, the pressures of her busy schedule and the young men in her life every once in a while. (Of course she would disagree with the last reason.)

We believe that teenagers need to know that their family is a rock for them, solid, through everything they face. When we are camping she knows whatever is going on in her life, she is accepted and loved. We are there to escape the chaos for a little while and to regain the strength to deal with our challenges. Sometimes, even though she doesn't want to come, we insist and she thaws enough to get the benefits of a rest, without ruining our vacation.

Megan shared her list of how to entice a teenager to camp with their parents. (You may detect some of her mothers' sarcasm near the end.)

1. Let them bring a friend or two, and set up a tent for them to sleep in.
2. Bring fun relatives.
3. Don't do boring stuff. You can't get away with vegging at the campsite with little kids for too long. Teenagers get bored. They need things to do, extreme things work best.
4. Let them help choose the destination and plan the trip. Waterslides, pools, rafting, horseback riding, and good hikes with worthwhile rewards like waterfalls or spectacular views at the end.
5. Bribe with candy and electronics.
6. Pay them.
7. Guilt trip (if all else fails).

About her #1

Because of the size of our family and the size of our trailer, we rarely bring friends. If one comes, though, we try to give them some privacy by setting up a tent where they can escape to talk and giggle all night. Hopefully they join us by the campfire and join the conversation, but if not, we let them do their thing. When she can't bring a friend, we let her keep in touch with her friends through texting, and that makes her less resentful of being away so she'll come visit with the relatives more.

About her #2

When bringing a friend isn't an option, we do try to camp with extended family or friends, including some fun adults who relate well to teenagers.

About her #3

As they get older, we can't just hang around the campsite and let the kids create their own fun because they get bored easily. We try to do more challenging activities that they can get excited about; whitewater rafting, horseback riding, skiing harder runs, challenging hikes with great views. If you are in a group paintball or other tournaments add excitement if your kids enjoy competition, like mine.

About her #4

We do get her input on activities and destinations, but we also get her involved by giving her other "fun" responsibilities. Megan's role as she got older was to read the ghost stories. She still reads "Scared but Silly" stories to the younger ones, but now she occasionally saves a good ghost story to share with the adults when the kids have gone in the trailer for the night. Last year, we used a passion she developed when she got a camera for her birthday and made her the official photographer of our trips. And of course she helps decide on and prepare our experiments for cooking over the fire.

As my son gets older, he is getting more involved. Since he took up whittling, I ask him to whittle things for the younger kids. This summer, along with whittling, he spends his time chopping wood and is learning to build good cooking fires. He is also becoming a writer and next year, I am hoping he will take over our RVing Journal.

About her #5

Not a chance

About her #6

Not a chance

About her #7

Whatever works . . .

RVing with Grandparents

The memories and stories that spill out of Oma, when we are sitting around the campfire, capture the grand-kids' imaginations and introduces them to another world, and the crazy idea that their parents, and even Oma, was their age at one time. RVing provides the relaxed together time needed for grandkids to become aware of their own history through their grandparents.

Camping with grandparents can be easy if they are healthy, independent and have their own RV. You may even get a break if they are willing to do something with the kids for a while. Any extra work required to bring more dependent or aging grandparents, though, is worth it. The resulting memories, and spontaneous shared experiences will help kids feel secure and encourage bonding with their future grandchildren.

Grandparents taking kids

Young healthy grandparents sometimes offer to take the kids camping to share their passion and give you a break. Although it is a wonderful opportunity to bond, if you want them to repeat the offer, consider these questions before you let kids go.

- Do the grandparents and kids know each other well enough?
- Are the kids a handlful even for you? Will they be too much for your parents, because your parents aren't used to kids anymore?
- Can you improve a child's behaviour for their grandparents, by making them realize it is a privilege?
- Can you let them go if they meet certain conditions like good grades, or better and more helpful behaviour at home? That is what will be expected if they are with their grandparents.
- Should you write up a contract with an older child including chores and behaviour expectations before you agree to letting them go?
- Should you divide the kids so grandparents only take one or two at a time?
- Should you only allow short holidays, or give grandparents flexible timelines, in case the kids end up being more than the grandparents can handle?
- Can you send toys that kids can use independently to give grandparents a break?
- Can you suggest activities or places that the kids might enjoy.
- Can you suggest that a nice gift from a teenager would be that they take the grandparents camping, except let the grandparents drive?

Keep them coming with you

Some grandparents don't feel comfortable or can't take the kids by themselves, but would agree to join you with their trailer or stay in a cabin near where you and your kids are RVing.

One way to keep those grandparents coming with you, is to ensure the children respect Grandma and Grandpa's needs and property. Keep the dialogue going. Ask the grandparents if they need more space.

As they get older, these grandparents may not be able to - or want to - handle the chaos and demands of busy children. They may need to keep the kids out of their trailer so they have a retreat or sanctuary when they are tired. Though they love to be in nature with their grandkids, they may need their independence, privacy and quiet routines to keep their balance. When they have had tea and a nap after lunch for 30 years, the stress of missing it may affect their health or well-being.

Physical challenges

As life takes its toll on their bodies, and it gets harder to move around, grandparents may need help to come. They may need someone to drive their motor home. They may need to drive shorter distances, or stop more often to move around or use the washroom. They may need help setting up, chopping wood, and dumping at the end of the trip.

Sharing meals

Having meals together with your family might be easier for the grandparents, but they probably can't eat some of the foods you eat, so consider this when making a menu and shopping.

Washroom woes

If there isn't a washroom in their recreation vehicle, you may want to rent a portable toilet to put in or just behind their trailer because seniors often need to use it in the middle of the night. If not, park near a washroom and give them a walkie-talkie to call you, in case they trip in the dark on their way.

Our 78-year-old Oma finds the showers in most campgrounds difficult to use because she has trouble bending over and she needs her special slippers to stop her from falling. We try to find campgrounds where she can use the handicap bathroom to shower. Some campground operators will give her permission and some leave the handicap washroom open. These washrooms have benches to sit down inside and outside the shower and handles to hang onto.

Hotel option

Another way you can bring aging grandparents is to camp in a campground located next to a hotel or lodging. It takes some searching, and it isn't quite the same as if they were out there with you, but if they can join you for breakfast, dinner and fires, it is quality time with them you wouldn't have at home with your busy life.

A cherished tradition - Oma's cafe

Our Oma, who is 78, still comes and keeps some traditions for her kids and her grandkids. Her grandkids will always remember "Oma's Café" as the place to which they stumble in their pajamas and with their blankets when they wake. They find us bundled in the fresh morning air, under a shelter that has Oma's homemade sign hanging from it, drinking her coffee. They crawl on our laps and wait for Oma to serve her famous hot chocolate and muffins. The tradition is being passed on, with her daughter running the cafe when we are winter camping without Oma, and someday, our kids will be inviting us to their trailer for our morning coffee and muffins.

Taking the family pets

Sadie knows when we are camping and she gets as excited as the kids. As soon as the trailer comes home, she hounds us (even though she is a Golden Retriever). She lays by the front door and dreamily stares at the trailer, making sure it doesn't leave without her. When I start to bring food and clothes into the trailer, she sits up tall on the front lawn, watching, waiting for us to hook up and pull our trailer onto the street. She knows the routine and knows when we're getting close.

Once the trailer is hooked up and on the street she won't leave us alone. She barks and flashes her puppy dog eyes everytime someone goes near the truck, and she runs back and forth with us as we load the last items into the car for the trip. Only when we open the back hatch and put her in her spot does she calm down. She won't let anyone take her out and will sit there for hours if we happen to have a glitch and can't go immediately. She is afraid to get out of the car: she doesn't want to be left behind.

At the campground she jumps out and starts exploring

with the kids, her nose to the ground, smelling all the interesting smells of wild animals.

Though this book's title is RVing with children, to many people, their pets are their children. Sadie is one of our family and an RV trip wouldn't be complete without her.

Sadie is a good RVing animal. She travels well and doesn't mind being on a rope or a leash which is required in many of the campgrounds. She doesn't bark too much and listens well. Having grown up around kids and other dogs, we never worry about her meeting other people or dogs. After diving for rocks in the nearest creek or river, or playing hide and seek with the kids or with the prairie gophers, she lays near us, content with being near her family. She lifts her head occasionally to give one lazy warning bark if any animal comes by, sure that that will be enough to protect her family and scare the animal away.

We are able to leave Sadie in the trailer with water and all the windows open on a hot day if we have to run into town. She has plenty of room but crawls on our bed and watches out the window, waiting for us and giving the dutiful bark if another animal comes too close. In the winter, when we go skiing, we only go for half days so she isn't left alone too long. We take her for a good run in the morning and she sleeps in the trailer all afternoon. If we are doing a trip that we know will find us away from the camper a lot, we leave her behind, letting her have a sleepover with her Oma and Opa.

There are extra things we need to do when Sadie is with us. Travelling with an animal requires more stops for water, exercise and bathroom breaks. In the RV Etiquette session, I talk about keeping your dog quiet and picking up after them. For safety, you must keep your dog food dishes in the

Sadie tests our CO Alarm

My husband is a safety guy. So when we bought our first hard-sided trailer for winter camping, he decided a smoke alarm, in case of fire and for my cooking, was not enough. We had to have a CO monitor in case we had a propane leak or a problem with the furnace.

It was the middle of January and the kids were still wide awake when we pulled in to the moonlit campsite at Tunnel Mountain in Banff. We were excited about having our first winter camping trip in our own trailer, but since it was nearing 11 p.m., we all fell asleep quickly with smiles of anticipation on our faces.

Around 3 a.m., a loud beeping woke my husband and I with a start. We shot from our bed to discover it was the CO alarm going off. I took a deep breath, smelled a familiar smell, and assumed it was propane or some sort of gas setting off the alarm. While my adrenaline level sky-rocketed, preparing my body to move the kids quickly out of the trailer, my eyes adjusted to the light and I spied Sadie. Her eyes turned from surprise to guilt, then she buried her face in her paws. My husband immediately realized what had happened. Lying in front of the CO monitor, Sadie's gas had set off the CO alarm!

trailer when you are not there, otherwise you will attract animals. You can leave water out, though. You also must keep pets on a rope or a leash. If a wild animal comes and they go and try to protect you, they may get hurt or come back with the animal in pursuit, putting you in danger. Being on a leash though, means they will need exercise or walks.

Make sure your pet is up to date on vaccinations and talk to your veterinarian about your trip. He may suggest other medicines such as one to prevent Lyme Disease from ticks, or he may have good reasons for you to consider leaving your pet at home.

Not every animal would like RVing. The long trips, the unfamiliar surroundings, smells and sounds, might disrupt a less inquisitive, flexible animal. I have also camped near dogs that barked constantly, panicking everytime their owners left them alone in the strange setting.

If Sadie could talk, I am sure she would tell you that, being outside, surrounded by her whole family all day and all night, is why she likes RVing so much. After all, we are her pack.

RVing with Groups or Clubs

Family reunions, weddings, a get-together of old friends and their families, and a soccer tournament are a few of the reasons we have gone group camping. We also get together with my husband's co-workers and their families for a company camping/golf weekend once a year. These gatherings can be lots of fun for kids and adults who are extroverts but for those who aren't that social, they can be trying. Here are a few tips:

Personal space

Crowds can tire kids out as well as adults. Respect other RVers' right to privacy and hold on to your privacy so you have a place for your family to retreat for a rest, quiet time after a meltdown or for time outs. We encourage the kids to play outside or in a play tent and try to visit with others in common areas.

Parking your RV

Where you park can make or break your group camping experience. If you aren't the first one at the group camping site you may not have a choice, but if you have a choice, consider your family's needs. '

Parking near the crowd

Because my husband and I are fairly social, if we know who we are camping with and feel comfortable with our kids and their behaviour, then we try to park with our door in sight of the firepit and not too far away. That way, once our kids are in the trailer for the night, we can still visit with others around the fire and watch out for our kids. Having four kids, all of our kids are used to sleeping through noise, so this works for us. If we are late and our RV is parked too far from the firepit, we drag the playtent near where we are visiting and let any tired kids bring their sleeping bags into the tent until we retire for the night.

Parking farther away

People who enjoy quiet time or who know their kids need quiet time may want to park further away from the crowd. Light sleepers should also park further from the campfire or common area. A disadvantage to parking further means someone has to stay in or near the trailer while small kids sleep. This can be a blessing and a perfect excuse if you want to steal some quiet time to read, avoid obnoxious people or go to bed early! If you need to go the firepit when the kids are sleeping for some reason, you may want to bring a battery-operated baby nursery monitoring system or walkie-talkies to keep in touch.

Winter gatherings

Park near a cookhouse and bring plastic and duct tape or staples to tarp off the windows and door. Once the fire is going and the kids are playing board games on the picnic tables, you'll feel like you're a pioneer holding a welcoming celebrating for rare visitors in a warm wooden cabin.

Picky eaters

When our kids were younger, they would not eat properly if they were surrounded by people or given food they weren't familiar with. They also didn't eat if they had a lot of distractions. If they didn't eat, they had meltdowns, so, until they could focus on their dinner around others, we had dinner in the trailer, or at a picnic table away from everyone.

Group Activities

To make the most of a group Rving experience, we try to plan some activities where the kids can get involved.

Tournaments

Tournaments where adults and kids can play together make the kids feel important. If there are very small kids we might have a bocce tournament, and let the kids join in. Even a two year old can play bocce, (use the novice or lighter bocce balls) but they do have to be supervised. A volleyball net, or plastic (safe) lawn darts are good if the kids are a little bit older. These activities are also not too stressful on out-of-shape adults.

Water fight

When the weather is hot, we schedule a special time for a water fight. That way, the kids have something to look forward to and they don't spray people all weekend. With a specific time set, you will have time to decide what you can afford to get wet, or will know when to put a bathing suit on. Of course, it is good to have rules like, if you don't have a gun or if you are refilling your gun, you can't get sprayed. This reduces fights, and lets the people that don't want to get wet off the hook.

Craft table

Set up a craft table where the kids can create while talking. It is a good way to help them socialize.

Cleansing swim

If you are camping near a town, and you have a good size group, you may want to rent the local pool. It is a great way to get all the kids clean and can be lots of fun.

Local attractions

If you are choosing a location, consider choosing one near special attractions for kids. A planned trip to a zoo, waterslide, science centre, paintball park for teens or horseback riding can give the kids something to look forward to and provide a break from watching the adults visit.

Sing-a-longs

Have musicians (or wannabes) bring their instruments and bring out the lyrics to some old favorites. Everyone can join in!

Booking a Group Site

If you are organizing one of these events, you will want to find a group camping spot well in advance. The spot should include these features.

Group privacy

At family reunions or other events, you may not know everyone who shows up, so you want some privacy, some physical barrier that lets people know this is a private group, to discourage people from walking through or assuming they can join in. It may be a private road entering an area surrounded by trees or you may have a loop with a field in the middle, with all of your group around it.

Picnic tables and garbage cans

Believe it or not, we booked a group campsite attached to a resort and they directed us to a field where we shared a cooking shelter with two other groups. There were no picnic tables, no washrooms, except half-a-kilometre away at the resort and no garbage cans. Make sure you ask what a group area includes.

Cookhouse

A cookhouse is an excellent option for shelter in case of bad weather. If it is really cold or windy, we put plastic up around the windows and fire up the stove. The room gets toasty and the kids play games on picnic tables, while we sit in our lawn chairs around the stove. If there is no cookhouse, put up a tarp to provide shelter if it rains or from the hot sun. You will probably need some picnic tables under the shelter.

Washrooms

Find out if they include sanitizer, paper towels and toilet paper. If they don't, you will want to bring your own.

Wood

If they don't provide the wood free, you may want to suggest that everyone bring a little bit from home.

Cooking

We have been group camping for years and tried a number of different group cooking strategies. My favorite is when people take turns cooking meals. For example, I have five siblings in my family and at a recent family reunion, we paired up with a sibling, and together with our families, we took responsibility for planning and feeding everyone one meal. Lunch was always leftovers. It was easy and fun and we weren't always cooking so we could enjoy our kids.

Hotels nearby

If you have seniors or people who don't or won't camp, they can still participate if they can stay nearby.

RV Clubs

Clubs for Everyone

RV Clubs are a great way to meet new people and socialize with like-minded individuals. Although some clubs are based on location, others are based on interests. There are family clubs, clubs for retired military, and clubs for RVers with different types of trailers, vehicles and motorbikes. There are elderhostel and adult-only clubs.

Benefits

Membership in a club can give you discounts at certain campgrounds, magazines, and invitations to rallies and tours. The biggest attraction for most people is the rallies. People come together and share in weekends of planned activities at a specific campground. These activities might include dances, group dinners, hikes, entertainment, competitions or tournaments. The Club may meet at the same place once a month or a different place every week.

Managing Risks

S taying one step ahead of my kids is a dance I am not always good at. I try to stay two steps ahead when it comes to protecting them from danger. Being in the wild has its dangers but common sense can protect our kids from many of them.

Cell phone range

If you are heading into the mountains, or away from civilization, check every once in a while to see if you have cell service or where it ends. If an emergency occurs, you need to know if cell service is close or not.

Be aware of emergency services in the area

In the wild, the nearest town's hospital may be too far to reach, but there may be a warden's office or firehall nearby where you can get help.

Winter fire hazard

When winter camping, ensure your electric heater has the safety shut-off feature if it tips over.

Lost kids

Ensure your kids know how to "Hug a Tree" if they become lost. The RCMP's "Hug a Tree" program is offered throughout the country and teaches kids what to do if they become lost. Among other things, they need to 'hug a tree' and stay put. Keeping warm and dry is important and they need to know that they won't be in trouble and should answer calls from searchers. There are many more tips on the Hug a Tree websites.

Setting boundaries

Boundaries can eliminate a lot of danger. Good boundaries keep kids from getting lost and hurt but don't stifle the imagination. When deciding the boundaries you will set for your kids, you need to consider a number of factors:

- intellectual, emotional and physical age of the child
- size of group you are in
- campground's population
- campground's layout
- local wild animals
- animals' habits
- recent sightings or signs of wild animals
- animals' seasonal challenges

Age of the child – Young children who watch Jungle Book may think that all animals are pets. They may think that because a cub is about the same size as their dog, they can go and pet it. They are not aware of the dangers of wild animals and can not protect themselves if confronted with one. The ability of a child to think in a crisis situation gets better with age and may be influenced by their personality type and maturity. You probably have a good idea of whether your child will panic, get too close or react wisely when confronted with a wild animal. Someone who is good in crisis situations may get more freedom than someone who panics easily. The size of the individual is also a consideration. Smaller children are easier prey and less intimidating to wild animals.

Size of group – A larger, louder group is always safer than a small one. We encourage the kids to ask the neighbours' kids to play and always tell them to stay together and watch for each other.

Campground's population – If you are in a remote location or in a fairly empty campground, you might want to keep the kids closer. In busy campgrounds we let our kids ride around the loop where we are parked. If they come across a wild animal and it is too dangerous to return, they have been told to run to the nearest open trailer for shelter. I find generally RVers are good people. There are very few ill-intentioned people who would make the effort to go camping, and the odds of my kids being attacked by a wild animal, or a dangerous criminal are higher with the wild animal.

Campground's layout – If there are steep cliffs or fast rivers nearby, shorten your boundaries on those sides. Thick bush is another element that can result in lost kids. We made roads our boundaries when we knew our kids didn't watch for cars.

Local wild animals – Typically, if you don't bother or feed wild animals and you give them space, they won't bother you. Of course there can be exceptions and so you need to stay close to your very young children and teach the older kids about the animals and how to protect themselves. Know what animals are found in the area you are RVing. Bears, cougars, elk and coyotes are some of the threats to children. Rattlesnakes and wolves may also be dangerous. Mosquitos carrying West Nile Disease have been found across the Canadian prairies and in Ontario as of 2007.

Animals' habits – Make a point of learning about the habitat and habits of the wild animals surrounding you. Do they usually sleep during the day? Do they like the tall trees or prefer fields full of berries or tall grass? Do they have an incredible sense of smell, sight, or hearing? How do they react when they are frightened? If a certain type of animal approaches, should you try to scare it and make yourself bigger, or freeze or back up slowly and quietly? How long and when do bears hibernate?

Recent sightings or signs of animals – Most campground officials will post signs and may even visit your campsite to let you know if a wild animal has been seen in the area. You should also look for scat, tracks, and fur on branches to let you know if this is a popular place for wild animals. If there is or was an animal in the area recently, we move our kids' boundaries closer.

Animals' seasonal challenges – Know when animals are most dangerous. Our kids' boundaries shrink if it is spring and there are new babies or if we can hear the bugling of elk in their fall rutting season. If berries were in short supply all summer and the only spot available for our fall camping trip was the middle of berry bushes, we leave or keep our kids really close. If the snow falls early, animals will come down from the alpine meadows to look for food.

Problem Bears

Bears which become accustomed to humans pose the largest risk to humans and themselves. Unfortunately, if they can find easy food they will take it and return often, becoming a problem bear. To keep humans safe, problem bears are trapped and removed from the area to a far off wilderness location. If they return again and again, they can be killed.

Therefore, all campgrounds follow strict rules about putting away food when you are not in your campsite. Food and cooking utensils should be in a locked hard-sided vehicle or tied high in a tree. Also, don't let kids wander off with food in their hands. Keep the food at the table.

Insects

A few mosquitos may carry West Nile Virus in Central Canada and the prairie provinces, but insects can cause allergic reactions anywhere, so protect your kids with a children's insect spray which includes deet (read instructions to see if it is suitable for your child's age) or cover them up with light-colored long sleeves and pants. We used netting to protect our babies in their playpen, stroller or chair. Citronella candles or mosquito-repellant coils can be lit nearby and gazebos with netting positioned over the picnic table can help save a bug-infested holiday.

If you have older kids who can handle the smoke, try this old farmers' trick. They throw grass on a fire to cause a smoky haze over their land. The smoke would keep the bugs down for the cows and it works for us.

Also, remind your kids that they should NOT touch any dead birds!!

Mother nature's threats

Heat/Sun – Sunburn, sunstroke, and dehydration are the enemy. Hats and sunscreen are two of our weapons, but I always have to remind myself to keep the kids hydrated. Babies are especially susceptible to dehydration. On very hot afternoons, we keep the kids out of the heat with a craft in the RV. Although we don't typically drink Gatorade or Powerade unless the kids are doing sports or are sick, I do allow it if the weather is extremely hot. Know the signs of and treatments for dehydration and sunstroke and seek medical help if it becomes severe. If your children are thirsty, cranky, weary, or complain of headaches and/or aches in the joints, hydrate them quickly because dehydration in kids progresses fast. If your kids have sunken eyes, fever, their skin doesn't bounce back quickly if you press it and they are vomiting or have diarrhea, it is time to get medical help.

Cold – When winter camping know the signs of and treatment for frostnip, frostbite and hypothermia. Kids sometimes have so much fun they don't want to come in. Frostnip usually affects areas that are exposed to the cold, such as the cheeks, nose, ears, fingers, and toes, leaving them white and numb. Frostnip can be treated with warm water. YOU need to test the water, because they can't feel the heat with frostnip and may burn themselves. Frostbite and hypothermia require immediate medical attention. Watch for hard pale and cold skin or if a person becomes confused or uncoordinated.

Tornado – RV's can be tossed in a tornado and the items in them can become projectiles. If you know a tornado is coming, find a solid structure to take shelter in, like the campground's bathroom or shower room. If you are driving, pull over, get out, lay in a ditch and put your hands over your head to protect it from flying debris.

Flash Flood – Do not drive through a flood. Two feet of fast flowing water can carry your RV away.

Lightning – Close your windows if you are in an RV and stay put.

Winter storm – If you are stuck in a winter storm, stay in your vehicle! Run the motor about ten minutes each hour and open the windows a little for fresh air. Make yourself visible to rescuers by turning on the dome light at night when running the engine. To avoid carbon monoxide poisoning make sure the exhaust pipe is not blocked. Once the snow has stopped tie a colored cloth to your antenna or door and raise the hood. Exercise as best you can to keep your blood circulating and to keep warm.

Hiking

Protection on the trail – When we hike with kids, we carry bear spray and both my husband and I know how and when to use it. If an animal attacks one of our children upwind, bear spray may hurt us more than the animal, so my husband also carries a knife to protect us.

To hike or not – When we had only one baby, as long as he was happy in the backpack, we hiked a lot. With two babies, it became tougher and then we realized we had to give up hiking for a short time. With four small children and two adults, we didn't feel we could pick them all up and run to safety if we encountered an animal or if someone had an injury, so we wandered through the campground if parks officials said there were no wild animals we needed to be worried about.

Hiking with children – Short day hikes on well populated trails are a good place to start with children. We motivate preschoolers with treats or water breaks if they count out a certain number of steps and by pretending we are a train or car. They can use their whistle, which is a safety tool that should be in every child's backpack, along with a garbage bag in case they get lost.

Some kids get tired and clumsy, injuring themselves if it's too far, and others want to run ahead, leaving you struggling to keep them in sight and out of danger. We never allow the kids to split up and the pace is always set by the slowest person - although we often carried the dawdler if the pace became painfully slow.

Generally, if you are hiking and you make enough noise, which we certainly do, no animal will come near and the larger group you hike in, the better.

Hiking with older kids – Older kids prefer to venture on more challenging hikes, offering scenic views, waterfalls, or rewarding climbing adventures. If you take more remote trails or overnight backpacks, make sure you let parks officials or family know where we are going. Make sure you keep hydrated and have energy food.

Cycling

Cycling – We have managed to continue biking through the kids' younger years. With a trail-a-bike (a bike with everything but the front wheel that attaches to our bike) and a bike trailer behind my husband's bike (some years with a car seat in it) and a bike seat on mine, we could still venture on longer trips like the well-marked trail next to the highway near Jasper, Alberta. For us, this trail always ended at Jasper's ice cream store. It doesn't take long before everyone can ride his/her own bike that far.

Cycling Rules – Our rules are to stay on well-marked trails, make lots of noise, and stay close to each other. We don't bike after dark and we go slowly around blind corners.

Bear Encounter on a Bike – Though we have never had the misfortune of running into a bear, we know that if we did encounter one at close range, we need to step off our bikes and walk slowly away, keeping the bikes between the bear and us. We don't try to outrun or out-cycle the bear and we don't try to go around him. We would back up, turn around and leave the area.

RV Resources

Friendly Businesses
No place to camp?If you are stuck with no place to park your RV overnight, Walmart Stores allow RVers to park overnight for free in their parking lots.

Forgot to Dump?
If you need to dump when you are away from the campground, all Canadian Tire stores have free dumping facilities on the side or back of their building. Tourist Information officers can also tell you of the nearest dump site.

Websites

www.gorving.ca
In Canada, GoRVing Canada provides a wonderful resource for Canadian RV Clubs, campgrounds, and technical tips.

www.RVHotlineCanada.com
This site has excellent articles and tips on driving RV's safely, winter camping, emergencies and more.

www.gorving.com
Travelling to the United States? Here is a website to help you

www.momsminivan.com
A great website with more ideas for travelling with kids is
www.momsminivan.com/

www.camping.about.com
If you are wanting to do more cooking over a fire, there are some great recipes on this website.

Workbook

Lists

* denotes things that stay in the trailer year round

NOTE: For kids' toys, you can't take it all. Pick and choose what your child would want.

Kitchen area

Cooking utensils*
Pots - big one for water and two others*
Pan and/or flat grill for over two burners*
Grill for over fire (with wire to adjust
  height if needed)*
Lids for all*
Handles (2) -if using camping pots*
Coffee pot, press or cup filter*
Insulated mugs (1/person)*
1-cup plastic measuring cup*
Corkscrew/can opener/bottle opener*
Oven mitts*
Juice pitcher*
Dish pan*
Cutlery in a portable container*
Steak knives*
Rubber spatula*
Wooden spoon*
Whisk*
Soup ladle*
Tongs*
Egg and pancake flipper*
Cheese grater*
Knives - paring and serrated*
Vegetable peeler*
Kitchen shears or scissors*
Cutting board*
Serving tray*
Two extra bowls, plates and glasses (hard
  plastic as a backup)*
Thermos*
Water bottles (1 per person)*
Electric Heater/fan* (if winter camping)

Lighter*
Flashlights*
Bearspray* (accessible)
Knife* (for whittling or protection)
Water Jug* (filled at home, especially in
  the winter for cooking)
Garbage can* (optional: we use grocery
  bags and hang them on cupboard han-
  dles)
Toaster* (to fit over gas burner)
Tin foil oven trays
Paper plates
Paper bowls
Plastic cutlery
Plastic glasses
Paper towel (lots)
Toothpicks
Tin foil cookie sheet
Zip loc bags
Tin foil (lots for crafts, too!)
Saran wrap
Paper towels
Plastic storage containers
Kitchen garbage bags
Green garbage bags
Dish soap
Hand sanitizer
Scratch pads
Dishcloths
Scrubber
Dish towels
Whisk and dust pan*
Vinyl tablecloth for picnic table*

Matches
Lighter fuel
Batteries (for flashlights)
Binoculars*
Mosquito coils or citronella candles
Baby nursery intercom system or walkie-
    talkies*
Sugar salt and pepper
Other preferred seasonings
Small container of flour (for paper mache
    or to seal painted rocks)
Backup Coffee

Tea
Chocolate milk mix
Gatorade mix
Chicken Noodle Soup packages
Kraft Dinner boxes
Brown beans

_____
_____
_____
_____

Outdoor gear

Cook stove*
Funnel*
Barbecue or Hibachi(optional)*
Rope (for clothesline, games, and tarp)*
Tarp*
Bungee cords*
Lantern*
Propane tree*
Lawn chairs*
Hammock*
Weiner sticks*
Gazebo with bug screens*
Cast-iron Sandwich maker*
Small cooler and backpack* for short

trips or picnics
Entry and Floor mats* (cover the floor for
    winter camping)
Folding dining table* (if no picnic tables)
Cook stove fuel
Propane or briquets (if you have your
    barbecue)
Lantern fuel
Plastic and staple gun (to cover windows
    in Cookhouse in the winter)

_____
_____
_____
_____

Tools

Axe*
Extension cord*
Wheel blocks*
Wrenches *
Pliers*
Screwdrivers *
Socket set*
Battery charger*
Collapsible shovel/saw*

Rubber gloves*
Drinking water hose*
Back-flush hose*
Rags*
Electrical and sewer hookups*
Blocks for parking*
Duct tape

_____
_____

Bedroom area

Sleeping bags*
Extra blankets*

_____
_____

Bathroom

Tweezers*
Nail clippers*
Q-tips
razors
Toilet paper (cheap 1-ply or recycled RV
    toilet paper)
Bath and/or Beach towels (we rent tow-
    els at pools)
Hand towels
Facecloths
Toothbrushes
Toothpaste
Anti-perspirants/deodorants
Make-up (optional)
Hairbrush and/or comb
Hair dryer
Bug spray, sun tan lotion
Shampoo/Conditioner
Tampons or pads
Spray cleaner
_____
_____

Medicine bag

First Aid kit with Bandaids, tape and
    bandages
Cleaning wound stuff
Tensor bandage
Polyporin
Vitamins/supplements
Adult painkiller and fever reducer
Anti-inflammatory
Children's painkiller and fever reducer
Children's anti-inflammatory
Imodium
Gravol
Lactaid (I have a lactose-intolerant child)
Personal medications
_____
_____

Shoe Tub

Sandals
Runners
Hiking boots
Winter boots
_____
_____

Clothes per person

___ pants
___ shorts
___ tank tops
___ short sleeve shirts
___ long sleeve shirts
___ sweaters
___ socks
___ underwear
___ long underwear

Outerwear

___ toques or hats
___ mittens and gloves
___ coats (fleece, rain, winter)
___ rain or snow pants
___ wool socks
___ sunglasses

Babies

Clothes
___Sleepers
___Warm jackets

___Fleece pants

_____

_____

Equipment

Chair to eat in*
Travel bed* (optional)
Umbrella stroller*
Playpen
Backpack
Snugli or sling
Netting for bugs
Waterproof mattress pad
Blanket
Teether*
Emergency soother*
Bottles, nipples and lids (one and a half
   day's supply)

Bottle liners
Breast pump
Baby spoons
Bibs
Extra soothers
Formula powder
Diapers
Wet ones
Few small toys or books

_____

_____

_____

_____

Toddlers (As needed from the baby section plus…)

Bear bell
Push toy
Balls
Buckets for collecting things
Pull ups

Potty
Blocks
Finger-rhyme books are great

_____

_____

Preschoolers (Also see baby, toddler & children section & craft box.)

Tricycles with push handles
Helmets
Bubbles
Tennis balls and Velcro pads
Balloons or punch balloons (to tie on a
   rope between trees)
Beach balls
Bocce (Novice set with lighter balls)
Waterguns

Glow sticks
Whistles
Pretend Steering wheels
Hot wheels tracks and cars
Dolls or stuffies (limit it)
Butterfly nets
Ziploc or bug containers

_____

_____

Children (Check the preschoolers' list and craft box too.)

Outdoor box
Tent for playing in*
Bikes, helmets and locks
Hockey sticks and tennis balls
Frisbees
Soccer/volleyball/basketball/football
Baseball, gloves and bat
Badminton racquets, net and birdies
Waterguns
Chalk
Rope
Nets
Bubbles

Skipping rope (long and short)
Roller blades, skateboards, or scooters
  (only if paved roads)
Safety gear (for above)
*Kids flashlights (one per person for
  nighttime tag)
Glow sticks (one per person
Telescope
Headlamps
Electronics

_____

_____

_____

Teenagers (By definition, teenagers are children one minute and adults the next, so check the children's list too.)

Electronics (They'll let you know what)
Camera or video camera
Whittling knives (in case you want to join
  him or her)*

Artists pad and drawing or painting
  materials
Books

_____

Pet (It's a dog in our case.)

Dish*
Long rope to tie her*
Leash*
Dog food
Toys or bone
Ball

Blanket
Medication
Towel or rag (for dirty paws)
Plastic bags
Booties (when winter camping)

_____

Lake trips

Lifejackets
Goggles
Snorkels
Beach balls
Sand toys
Blow up toys
Water shoes

Nets and containers to catch minnows or
  collect shells
Children's fishing rods (without hooks to
  practice casting)
Inflatable boat

_____

_____

Extra Winter Gear

Hockey sticks
Pucks/Tennis balls
Skates
helmets (skate or ski)
skis
harnesses

poles
toboggans
garden shovels (small)

_____
_____
_____

Indoor Craft box

Painter's tape
Tape
Popsicle sticks
Homemade play dough
Toothpicks (for creating small marshmal-
   low crafts)
Pipe cleaners
Construction paper
Crayons or markers
Scissors
Boxes
Rock paint
Paint brushes

Sticky foam pieces
String or elastic
Play dough
Glue (I only let them use that outside)
Foam stickers Beads or string for friendship
   bracelets and jewellery
Balloons (WARNING: keep them in a safe
   place if there are little kids)
NOTE: You can also use paper plates, bowls,
   and plastic glasses, tin foil and empty
   containers from your recycling bag

_____
_____

Books

Camping Journal*
Ghost stories*
Bug and insect reference book (This is
   the most popular in our trailer)*
Animal reference book*
Bird reference book*
Wildflower, bush & tree reference books*

Survival book*
Book of skipping songs*
Book of lyrics for campfire songs*
Finger play rhymes for babies*

_____
_____

Board Games (If space is an issue just bring the cards of trivia-type games.)

Playing Cards
Yahtzee

Extra Dice
Puzzles

Car Box List

Extra vehicle keys
Trailer registration and insurance
Parks pass or RV Club card (if required)
Map
Band aids and polysporin
Towels (on seat)
Wet ones
Paper towels

kleenex
Ziploc bags
Garbage bags
Earplugs (?)
Coat and shoes for each child

_____
_____
_____

For Babies

Diapers
Pull-ups
Extra bottle(s)
Connecting rings leash

Extra pacifier
Pacifier clip to attach to clothes

_____
_____

Snacks bag may include

Sausage and cheese(bring knife)
Bagels and cream cheese
Pre-made sandwiches
Grapes (cut up for babies)
Mandarin oranges
Water bottles
Small juice boxes or bottled juice with
screw on top

Chips (Stacked chips to save space)
Smarties
Liquorice
Cookies

_____
_____
_____
_____

Miscellaneous

Baby bribery bag
-small toys (nothing they can choke on)
-small books (mine like the flaps)
-finger rhyme book
Electronics with relevant software
Portable DVD Player
Power bar
Power converter
Speakers and/or headphones

Kids' car bags
-small favorite toys\
-favorite books
-activity books
-sketch pad
-pencil and pencil crayons
-eraser and pencil sharpener
-other things they choose

_____
_____
_____

_____
_____
_____

Menu & Grocery Lists

MENU: 3-day Summer Camping Trip

We often use cereal as a snack and don't eat lunches all the time.

3 Breakfasts
Sausage, toast and yogurt or cereal
Bacon and pancakes or eggs
Bagels and cream cheese (trip home)

3 Lunches
Buns, ham and cheese
Taco salad
Hot dogs or beans and weiners

3 Dinners
Corn cob & baked potatos & steak (on the fire)
Roast, ceasar salad and garlic bread (left
  over potatoes maybe)
Pizza

3 Desserts
Turnovers
Barbecued Peaches with brown sugar
S'mores in a cone

Grocery Lists

Breakfasts

Sausage	Pancake mix	Coffee
Bread	Milk (Homo and 1%)	Sugar
Cheese whiz	Lactaid milk	Sweetner
Dutch cheese	Eggs	Hot chocolate mix
Peanut butter	Pancake syrup	Juice
Yogurt	Margarine	Oranges
Cereal	Jam	_____
Bacon	Bagels	_____
Ketchup	Cream cheese	_____

Lunch

Cheese slices	Mustard	Taco chips
Ham slices	Brown beans	Catalina dressing
Buns	Taco meat (pre-cooked)	_____
Sub sauce	Lettuce	_____
Hot dogs	Cheddar cheese	_____
Hot dog buns	Tomato	_____

Dinner

Corn cobs
Salt
Potatoes
Sour cream
Bacon bits
Onion
Steak

Steak spices or marinade
Barbecue sauce
Mayonnaise
Roast (pre-cooked)
Ceasar Salad (package
    with dressing and crou-
    tons)

Parmesan cheese
French loaf
Garlic
_____
_____
_____
_____

Desserts/Treats

Turnovers
Freezies
Brown sugar
Canned peach halves
Bananas

Chocolate chips (small
    container)
Mini marshmallows (craft,
    snack and hot chocolate)
Ice cream cones

_____
_____
_____
_____

Snacks

Sausage
Cheese
Crackers
Tortilla Chips
Salsa
Cheese dip
Flour mix for bannock

Grapes
Oranges
Canned Fruit cups
Cookies
Chips (stacked)
Liquorice
Granola bars

Nuts or GORP (good old
    raisins and peanuts)
Pudding
Juice boxes
_____
_____
_____

Other drinks

Pop
Baileys (for coffee)

Pre-made Ceasar's
Corona

Lime juice
_____

Menu & Grocery Lists

MENU: 3-day Winter Camping Trip

3 Breakfasts
Buns, eggs and cheese
Sausage, toast and yogurt or cereal
Bacon and frozen waffles or eggs

3 Lunches
Soup and grilled cheese sandwiches
Beans and wieners
Macaroni and Cheese with sausage

3 Dinners
Frozen Lasagne, Ceasar salad and garlic bread
Frozen Chicken wings, Perogies and brown beans
Swedish Meatballs, with sauce, rice and corn

Grocery Lists

Breakfasts

Buns
Cheese Slices (lunch and breakfast.)
Ham slices Eggs
Ketchup
Sausage
Bread
Cheese whiz
Dutch cheese

Peanut butter
Yogurt
Cereal
Milk (Homo and 1%)
Lactaid milk
Bacon
Frozen waffles
Syrup
Margarine

Jam
Coffee
Sugar
Sweetner
Hot chocolate mix
Juice
Oranges

_____

Lunch

Chicken Noodle Soup packages
Brown beans (enough for lunch and dinner)

Hot dogs
Kraft Dinner
Ham Sausage Ring

_____
_____
_____

Dinner

Frozen lasagne (must fit
  in oven)
Ceasar Salad (package with
  dressing and croutons)
Parmesan Cheese
Bacon bits

Garlic Bread
Frozen Chicken wings
Perogies
Sour Cream
Frozen Swedish
  Meatballs
Sauce (pre-made)

Instant Rice
Creamed corn

_____
_____
_____
_____

Desserts/Treats/Snacks

Turnovers
Brownies (from home)
Nuts or GORP (good old
  raisins and peanuts)
Cookies
Sausage

Cheese
Crackers
Tortilla Chips
Salsa
Cheese dip
Grapes

Oranges
Canned Fruit cups
Chips (stacked)
Liquorice
Granola bars
Pudding

Other liquids

Pop
Baileys (for coffee)

Pre-made Ceasar's
Corona

Lime juice
Wine (tetra-pack)

Index

Acknowledgements

My teenager thinks my fifth baby is my computer, because I "freak out" anytime anyone touches it. She's wrong. This book is my fifth baby.

And I have had so much support bringing it to life. Thank you to my family for all their support and patience, and for sharing the adventures which led to this book. To my Writing Group; Audra Hollingshead, Kelly Klapstein, Carol Moore and Erin Shaw, who kept me inspired, focussed and helped me conquer writer's blocks and bad grammar throughout the gestation period, thank you. Lois, thanks for your support and feedback. Monica, thanks for swapping kids with me so I would have time to write and for rescuing me when my printer burnt out. And finally, thank you to Dean Pickup, the graphic designer/midwife (midhusband?) who made my baby pretty for it's delivery.

Joan van Dolder